WORLD HISTORY
THE HUMAN EXPERIENCE

Mapping History Activities

NATIONAL GEOGRAPHIC SOCIETY

Mounir A. Farah

Andrea Berens Karls

GLENCOE
McGraw-Hill

New York, New York   Columbus, Ohio   Woodland Hills, California   Peoria, Illinois

Customize Your Resources

No matter how you organize your teaching resources, Glencoe has what you need.

The **Teacher's Classroom Resources** for *World History: The Human Experience* provides you with a wide variety of supplemental materials to enhance the classroom experience. These resources appear as individual booklets accompanied by a file management kit of file folders, labels, and tabbed binder dividers in a carryall file box. The booklets are designed to open flat so that pages can be easily photocopied without removing them from their booklets. However, if you choose to create separate files, the pages are perforated for easy removal. You may customize these materials using our file folders or tabbed dividers.

The individual booklets and the file management kit supplied in **Teacher's Classroom Resources** give you the flexibility to organize these resources in a combination that best suits your teaching style. Below are several alternatives:

- **Organize all resources by category**
  (all Tests, all Geography and History Activities, all History Simulations, and so on, filed separately)
- **Organize resources by category and chapter**
  (all Chapter 1 activities, all Chapter 1 tests, etc.)
- **Organize resources sequentially by lesson**
  (activities, quizzes, study guides, etc., for Section 1, Section 2, and so on)

Glencoe/McGraw-Hill
A Division of The McGraw-Hill Companies

Copyright © by the McGraw-Hill Companies, Inc. All rights reserved. Permission is granted to reproduce the material contained herein on the condition that such material be reproduced only for classroom use; be provided to students, teachers, and families without charge; and be used solely in conjunction with *World History: The Human Experience*. Any other reproduction, for use or sale, is prohibited without prior written permission of the publisher.

Send all inquiries:
Glencoe/McGraw-Hill
936 Eastwind Drive
Westerville, OH 43081

ISBN 0-02-823237-2

Printed in the United States of America
5 6 7 8 9 10   045   02 01 00 99

MAPPING HISTORY ACTIVITIES

TABLE OF CONTENTS

To the Teacher		iv
Chapter 1	Humans Migrate and Produce Food	1
Chapter 2	The Kingdoms of the Fertile Crescent	2
Chapter 3	Canaan	3
Chapter 4	The Wanderings of Odysseus	4
Chapter 5	The Empire of Alexander the Great	5
Chapter 6	Barbarians at the Borders	6
Chapter 7	Trade Across North Africa	7
Chapter 8	Trade with the East and West	8
Chapter 9	Expansion of Empire: Han Conquests from 141 B.C. to 42 B.C.	9
Chapter 10	Justinian's Conquests	10
Chapter 11	Distant Outposts	11
Chapter 12	The Walking Word	12
Chapter 13	France in A.D. 1400s	13
Chapter 14	Languages of East and Southeast Asia	14
Chapter 15	Who Took What?	15
Chapter 16	The Success of Reform	16
Chapter 17	Routes of Trade and Cultural Exchange	17
Chapter 18	The Taiping Rebellion	18
Chapter 19	The Hapsburg Empire	19
Chapter 20	The Age of Revolution	20
Chapter 21	Saratoga: Turning Point of the War for Independence	21
Chapter 22	The French Revolution	22
Chapter 23	The Domestic System and Water Transportation	23
Chapter 24	The Voyage of the *Beagle*	24
Chapter 25	The Expanding United States	25
Chapter 26	The Economy of Austria-Hungary	26
Chapter 27	Africa's Natural Resources	27
Chapter 28	World War I in the Balkans	28
Chapter 29	Movements of People 1919–1939	29
Chapter 30	The Long March	30
Chapter 31	War on a Global Scale	31
Chapter 32	Europe Divided	32
Chapter 33	Agriculture in China	33
Chapter 34	African Vegetation	34
Chapter 35	Who's Got the Oil?	35
Chapter 36	Travels of a Revolutionary	36
Chapter 37	The Commonwealth of Independent States	37
Answer Key		38
Acknowledgments		44

To the Teacher

Mapping History Activities provide students with the opportunity to analyze and interpret maps. Students will answer questions that require them to use information given on the map. Many of the activities require them to find distances between places shown on the map or to add other information to the map.

Answers to the activities are provided at the back of the booklet.

Name _____ Date _____ Class _____

MAPPING HISTORY Activity 1

Humans Migrate and Produce Food

The earth has experienced several Ice Ages separated by long periods of warming. The climatic changes caused by the Ice Ages prompted early humans to migrate to new land areas. The map below shows their routes. Use it to complete the questions and activity that follow.

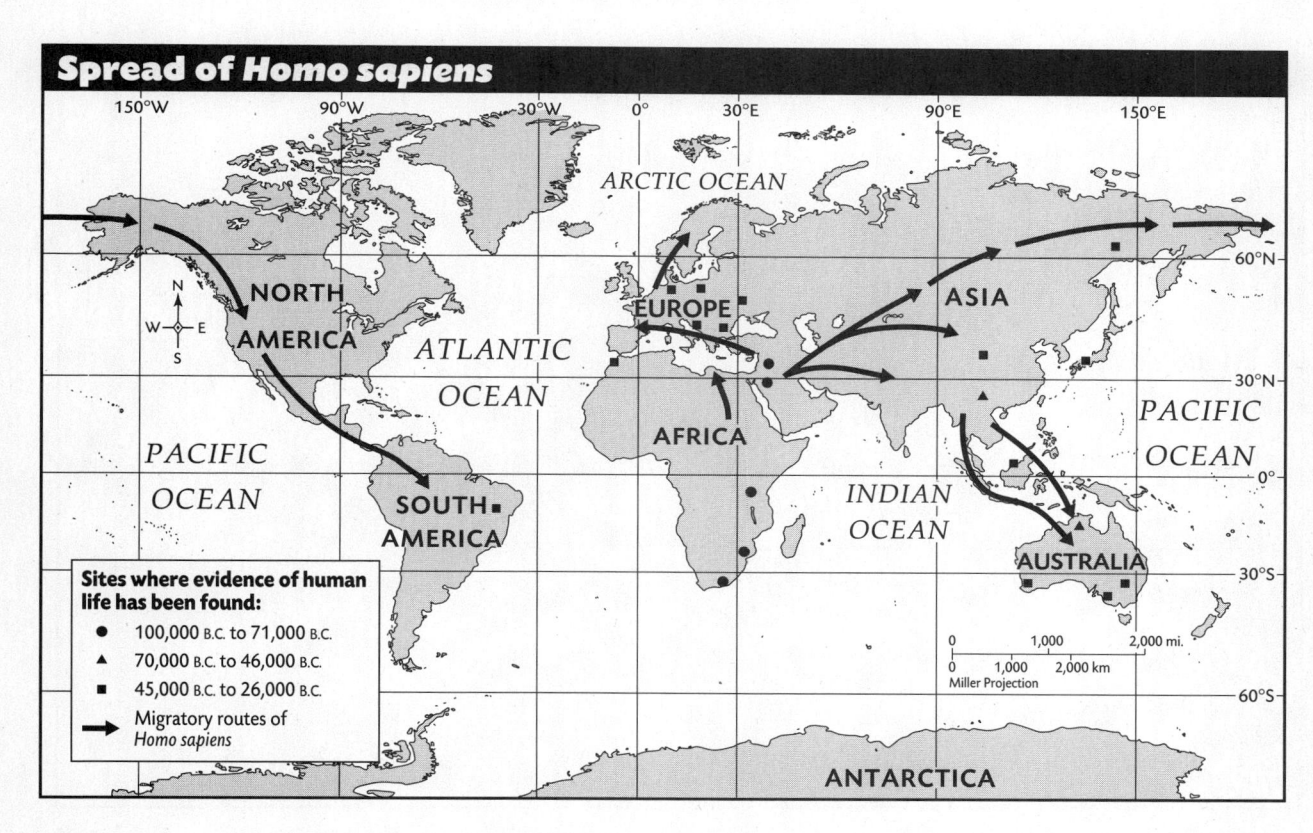

Spread of Homo sapiens

Sites where evidence of human life has been found:
- ● 100,000 B.C. to 71,000 B.C.
- ▲ 70,000 B.C. to 46,000 B.C.
- ■ 45,000 B.C. to 26,000 B.C.
- → Migratory routes of Homo sapiens

1. Where has evidence of *Homo sapiens* been found that dates between 100,000 and 71,000 B.C.?
   _____

2. Describe the route that *Homo sapiens* took from the Middle East to South America. _____
   _____
   _____

3. Since the last Ice Age, human population has tremendously increased, largely due to the development of agriculture. Agriculture began with the domestication of native plants and animals, including watermelon and rice in West Africa; bananas, cucumbers, and yams in Southeast Asia; cattle and grapes in southern Europe; soybeans in China; camels in Central Asia; avocados, maize, and tomatoes in Central America; and turkeys, sunflowers, and beans in North America. Revise the map above to show where these plants and animals were first domesticated. Create symbols for the plants or animals and add a map key to explain them.

World History | Mapping History Activities | 1

Name _____ Date _____ Class _____

MAPPING HISTORY Activity 2

The Kingdoms of the Fertile Crescent

The Fertile Crescent, which ran between the Tigris and Euphrates Rivers, was the site of a number of advanced cultures. The map below shows the kingdoms of the Fertile Crescent. Use it to answer the questions and complete the activities that follow.

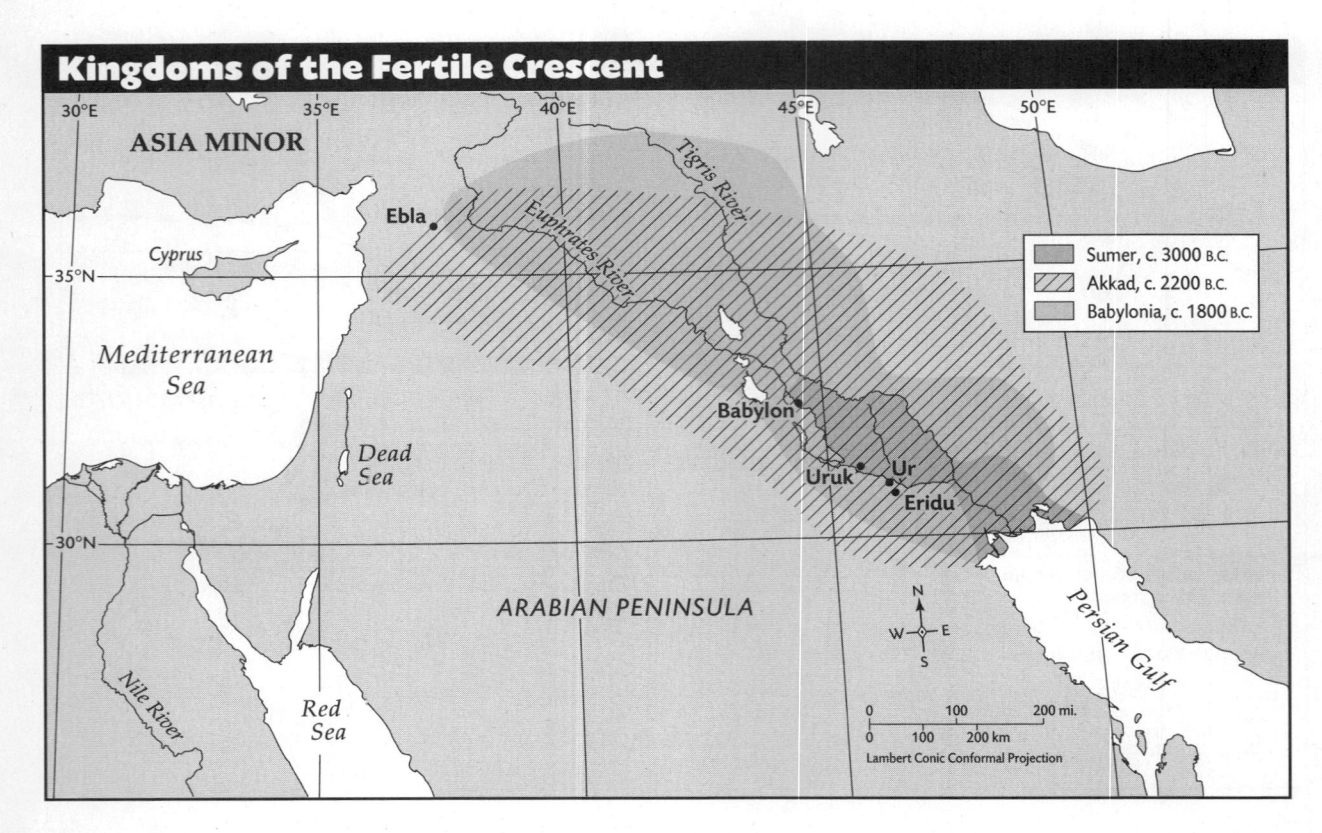

Kingdoms of the Fertile Crescent

Legend:
- Sumer, c. 3000 B.C.
- Akkad, c. 2200 B.C.
- Babylonia, c. 1800 B.C.

1. Which city-state lies closest to the Persian Gulf? _____
2. Which city-state lies closest to the Mediterranean Sea? _____
3. In which kingdom were the city-states of Ur and Uruk located? _____
4. Use the map scale to add the following information to the map:
   a. The city of Kish was 50 miles east of Babylon.
   b. Issin was 100 miles southeast of Babylon.
   c. Addab was 75 miles due east of Issin
   d. Larsa was 200 miles downriver from Babylon.
   e. The cities you added to the map were part of which empire? _____

2   Mapping History Activities   World History

Name .... Date .... Class ....

MAPPING HISTORY Activity 3

Canaan

Around 3000 B.C., the Phoenicians, a Semitic group, migrated from the Arabian Peninsula and settled in the northern part of Canaan, where they joined the Philistines. Just over one thousand years later, Israelite Abraham and his followers left the Mesopotamian city of Ur and settled in Canaan. The Israelites left Canaan when a severe drought caused a terrible famine. The map below shows Canaan. Use it to complete the activities that follow.

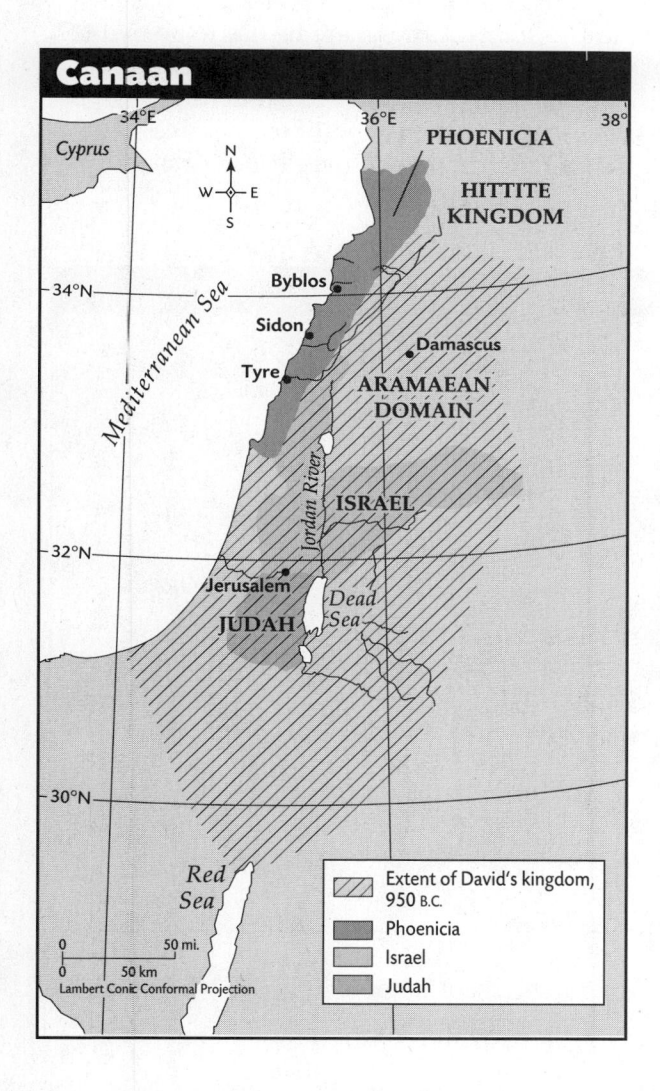

Canaan

[Map showing Canaan with labels: Cyprus, Phoenicia, Hittite Kingdom, Byblos, Sidon, Tyre, Damascus, Aramaean Domain, Mediterranean Sea, Jordan River, Israel, Jerusalem, Dead Sea, Judah, Red Sea. Legend: Extent of David's kingdom, 950 B.C.; Phoenicia; Israel; Judah. Scale: 0–50 mi / 0–50 km. Lambert Conic Conformal Projection.]

1. Based on this map, why do you think the Phoenicians became sailors?

   _____
   _____
   _____

2. Use the compass rose to describe the location of Cyprus in relation to Jerusalem.

   _____
   _____
   _____

3. To which kingdom did Tyre belong?

   _____

4. About how many miles long and wide did David's kingdom extend in 950 B.C.?

   _____
   _____

5. On the map, draw a route the Phoenicians could have traveled from the northernmost tip of the Red Sea to Byblos. Then use the scale on the bottom of the map to calculate the number of miles the Phoenicians would have traveled along this route.

   _____

World History   Mapping History Activities   **3**

Name .... Date .... Class ....

MAPPING HISTORY Activity 4

The Wanderings of Odysseus

After the battle of Troy, Odysseus wandered for ten years. The map below shows the lands he traveled through. Use it and the passage below to complete the activities that follow.

In Homer's *Odyssey*, Odysseus and his crew first sail from Troy to the land of the Lotus-Eaters. He then sails north and blinded a huge one-eyed monster, the cyclops Polyphemus, before encountering the Laestrigonians, a terrible race of giant-men who devours many members of the crew. Afterward, the goddess Circe turns many of Odysseus's men into pigs but aids Odysseus in contacting past heroes at the entrance to the underworld. Odysseus continues southward, where he has to be tied to the mast of his ship to avoid giving in to the beautiful songs of the Sirens. After steering clear of the six-headed Scylla and the whirlpool named Charybdis, the starving crew dares to eat the cattle of the sun god Hyperion on the island of Helios. Only Odysseus escapes to the island of the goddess Calypso, who keeps him prisoner. Finally, Odysseus builds a raft and sails to the Phaeacians, and then home to Ithaca.

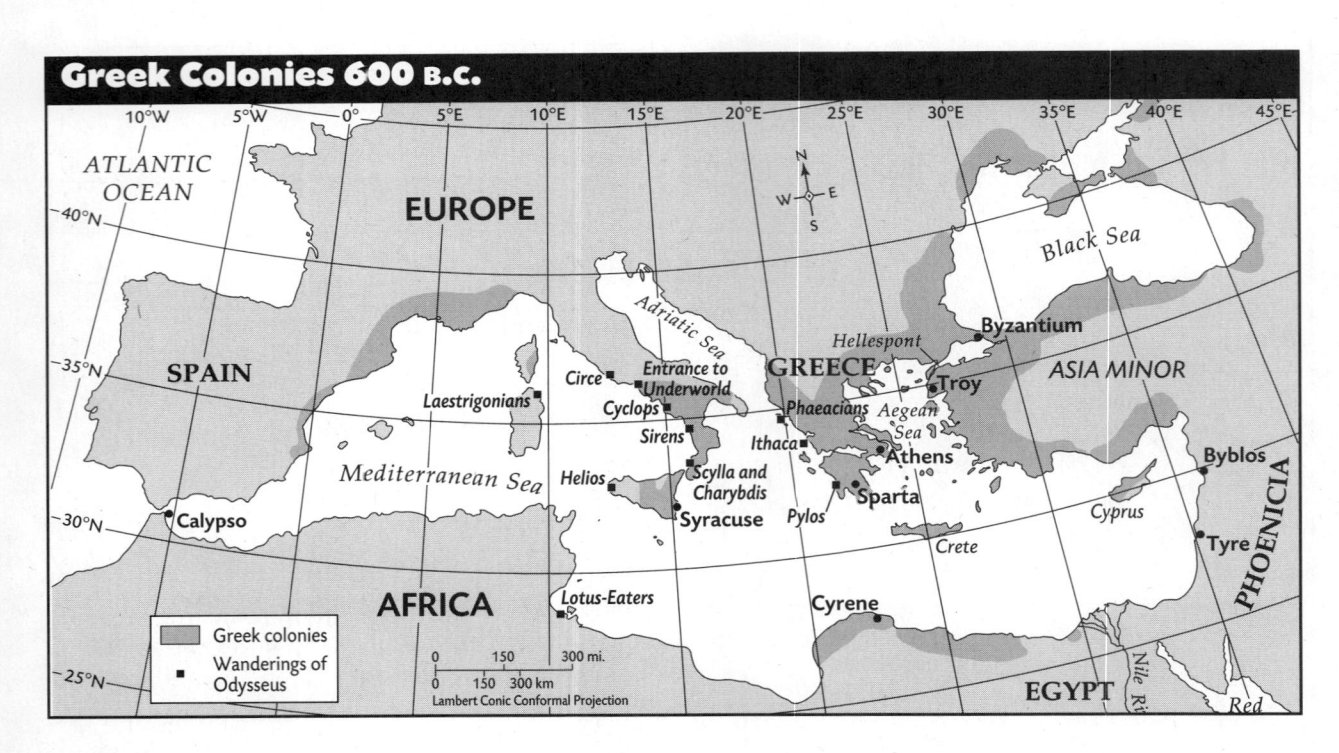

Greek Colonies 600 B.C.

1. What is the straight-line distance from the city of Troy to Odysseus's home in Ithaca? _____
2. Which part of Odysseus's trip covered more territory: from Troy to the land of the Lotus-Eaters, or from Scylla and Charybdis to Calypso's island? _____
3. Use the information in the passage to draw a line charting the course that Odysseus took on his long travels home. Add arrows to show his direction of travel along the line.
4. What is the longest distance between two points on Odysseus's travels? _____
5. What is the shortest leg of Odysseus's travels? _____

4   Mapping History Activities   World History

MAPPING HISTORY Activity 5

The Empire of Alexander the Great

At the height of his empire, Alexander controlled a vast stretch of territory from Macedonia in the west to Alexandria Eschate in the east. The route that Alexander and his army took to win control of the region was complex, and frequently they retraced their steps—sometimes several years later. The map below shows the route Alexander followed. Use it to complete the activities that follow.

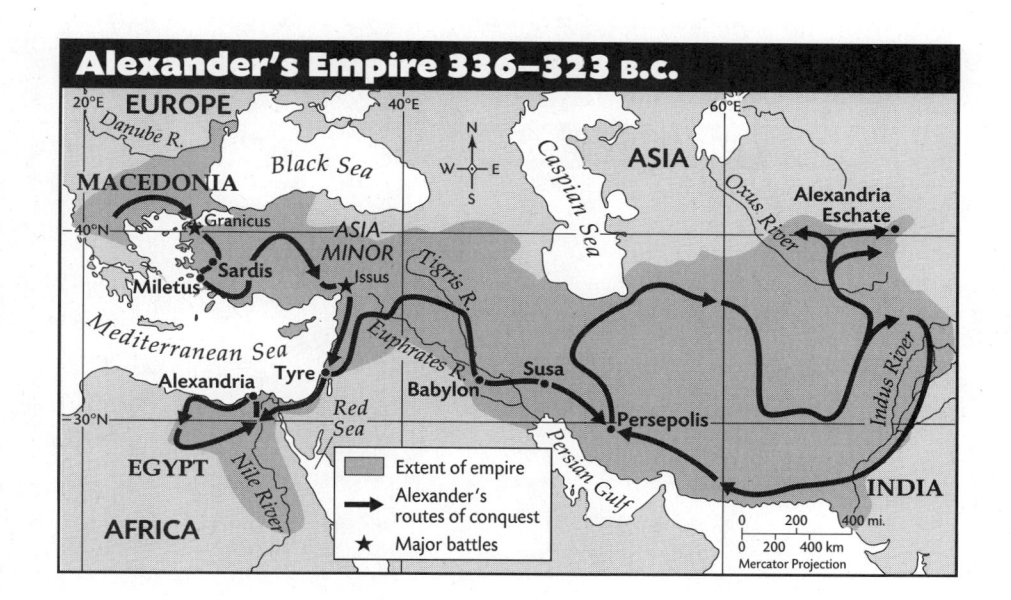

Alexander's Empire 336–323 B.C.

1. What is the approximate distance covered by Alexander's troops on their journey from Tyre to Persepolis? _____

2. From Tyre to Persepolis, how many times did Alexander cross the Tigris River? _____

3. On what continents did Alexander travel? _____

Use the information below and an atlas to map the domains of Antigonius, Ptolemy, and Seleucus. You may wish to use a different pattern of lines or a different color for each of the domains. If so, add a key to the map to show how you represent each domain.

After the death of Alexander the Great, three of his generals divided his empire into three separate domains as follows:

Antigonius: Macedonia and Greece

Ptolemy: Egypt, Libya, and western Syria

Seleucus: Eastern Syria, Mesopotamia, Iran, and Afghanistan

4. Following Alexander's death, which general had the largest amount of territory? _____

5. Which general had the smallest amount of territory? _____

Name .... Date .... Class ....

MAPPING HISTORY Activity 6

Barbarians at the Borders

Throughout its history as a republic and an empire, Rome faced the problem of invasion by foreign tribes. They came seeking a warmer climate, better land, a share of Rome's wealth, and safety from other tribes. It was not until about A.D. 200, however, that these invasions began to pose serious threats to the empire as a whole. By the A.D. 400s, invaders had attacked Italy and even the city of Rome itself, contributing significantly to the fall of the Roman Empire. The map below shows the Germanic invasions. Use it to complete the activities that follow. Write your answers on a separate sheet of paper.

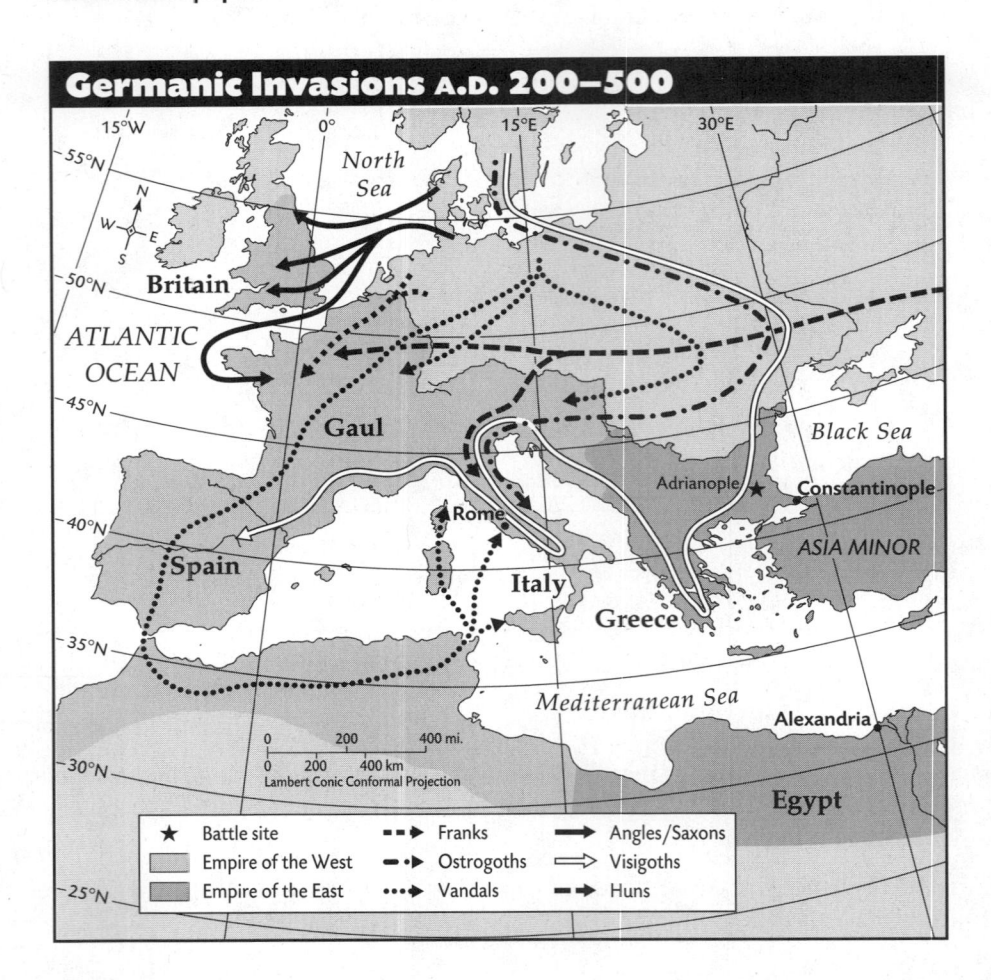

Germanic Invasions A.D. 200–500

(Map showing invasion routes of Franks, Ostrogoths, Vandals, Angles/Saxons, Visigoths, and Huns across Europe and the Mediterranean, with labels for Britain, Atlantic Ocean, Gaul, Spain, Italy, Rome, Greece, Adrianople, Constantinople, Asia Minor, Black Sea, Mediterranean Sea, Alexandria, Egypt, North Sea. Legend: Battle site, Empire of the West, Empire of the East, Franks, Ostrogoths, Vandals, Angles/Saxons, Visigoths, Huns.)

1. Which tribe came from Asia?
2. Which four tribes invaded Italy?
3. Which two tribes actually invaded Rome?
4. Which tribe crossed the Mediterranean Sea?
5. Many Roman colonies, or military outposts, are cities today. Use a map of modern-day Europe to locate these Roman colonies and add them to the map: Eburacum (York), Londonium (London), Bonna (Bonn), Singidunum (Belgrade), Magontiacum (Frankfurt), Siccia (Vienna), Olisipo (Lisbon), Aquincum (Budapest).

Name _____ Date _____ Class _____

MAPPING HISTORY Activity 7

Trade Across North Africa

Around the year A.D. 1000, African civilizations flourished. As their wealth increased, they began to establish trade routes to exchange their products for goods that they were unable to produce themselves. In particular, the kingdoms of West Africa grew rich because of trading. The most important city in this continental trade was Timbuktu, which then became a center for learning and Islamic scholarship. Use the map below to complete the activities that follow.

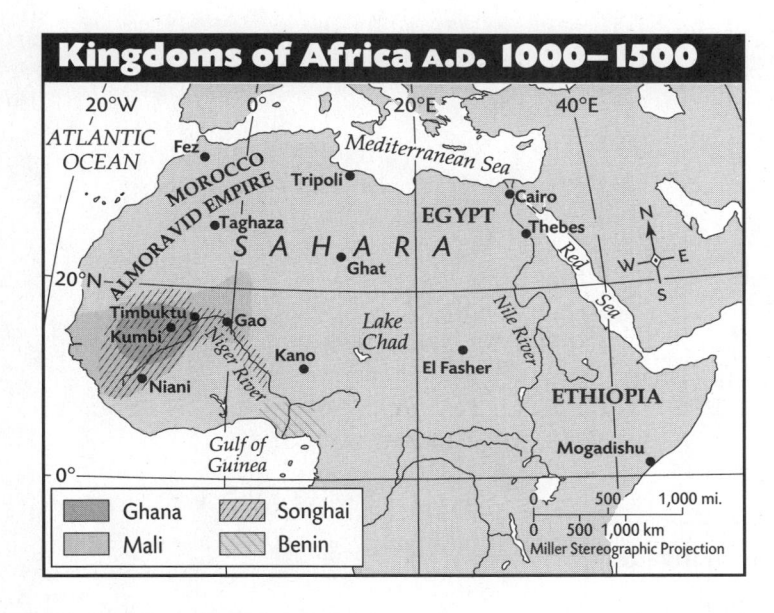

Kingdoms of Africa A.D. 1000–1500

1. Timbuktu was a city found in which kingdoms? _____
2. Which waterway was most important for the people of Timbuktu? _____
3. Name the important port cities of Northern Africa. _____

Read the following historical description of North African trading. Using the information provided in the paragraph, add arrows to the map above to indicate trade routes.

Salt was so common in the village of Taghaza that houses were built out of it. The people of Timbuktu needed salt to preserve and flavor food. It was also necessary for good health, since in hot climates, the human body loses salt through perspiration. The people of North Africa wanted gold, which was very plentiful in the area called Waranga located south of Niani. Timbuktu grew rich because it was about halfway between Waranga and Taghaza. Merchants came to Timbuktu to exchange salt for gold.

Other trade routes opened up as well. European goods were imported into Africa via Fez, where merchants from Timbuktu and Taghaza traded gold for them. Other traders traveled down the Niger River and then to Kano and El Fasher, before traveling down the Nile to buy Asian goods arriving at the port of Cairo. Asian goods coming from the Middle East were also shipped along the Mediterranean coast to Tripoli, where merchants coming from Timbuktu via Ghat came to trade.

World History   Mapping History Activities **7**

Name _____ Date _____ Class _____

MAPPING HISTORY Activity 8

Trade with the East and the West

During the Mauryan and Gupta Empires, Indian traders visited many places throughout the world in an effort to sell goods such as cotton, ivory, brass, elephants, and parrots. The map below shows these places. Use it to complete the activities that follow. Write your answers on a separate sheet of paper.

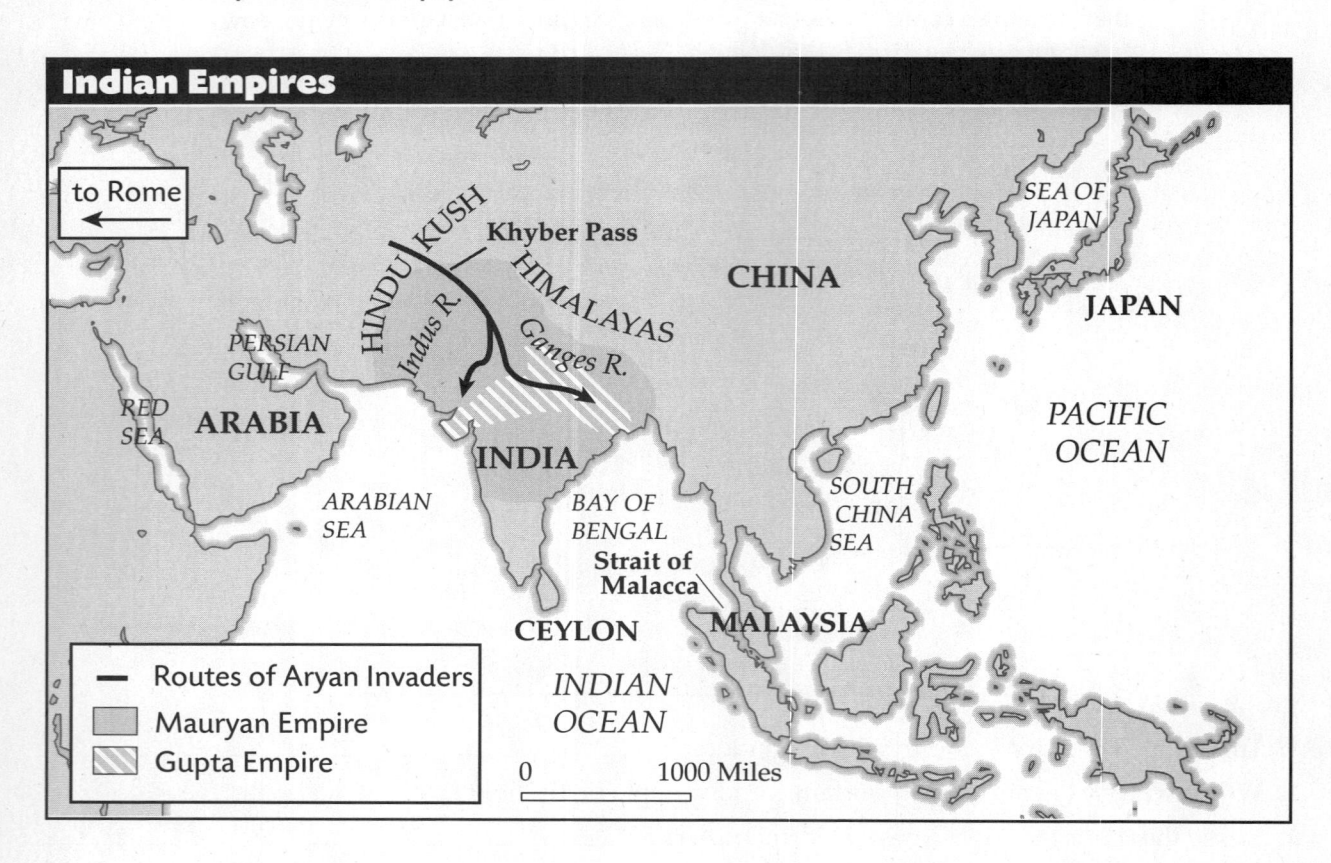

Indian Empires

- — Routes of Aryan Invaders
- Mauryan Empire
- Gupta Empire

0   1000 Miles

1. How do you think Asoka's legal system might have helped today's historians piece together the size of his empire more than 2,000 years ago?
2. What large natural feature did both empires contain, and why is it important to the survival of any civilization?
3. What does the path of the Aryan invaders, along the major river valleys, tell you about the land in between those rivers?
4. Now draw the trade routes linking India with Southeast Asia and China to the east and with Rome and Arabia to the west. Indian traders traveling to China by sea began in the Bay of Bengal and traveled south to Ceylon (now Sri Lanka). Then they sailed east toward Malaysia and through the South China Sea. An overland route through Central Asia also existed. To get to Rome and Arabia, Indian traders traveled through the Khyber Pass in the Hindu Kush Mountains.

Name .... Date .... Class ....

Mapping History Activity 9

Expansion of Empire: Han Conquests from 141 B.C. to 42 B.C.

The Han went to war in order to safeguard both their home provinces and their vulnerable trading routes in northwestern and central Asia. Under Wudi, Han armies successfully beat the Hsiung-nu, a nomadic race living to the northwest who harassed northern China and controlled parts of the trade route leading to the west. The Chinese government established colonies in the newly-won areas; in fact, the Han extended the Great Wall westward as far as the "Jade City" or Yumen. Oases around the Tarim Basin, which the Silk Road circled, were quickly put under Han protection to ensure the longevity of the trade routes. Use the map below to complete the activities that follow.

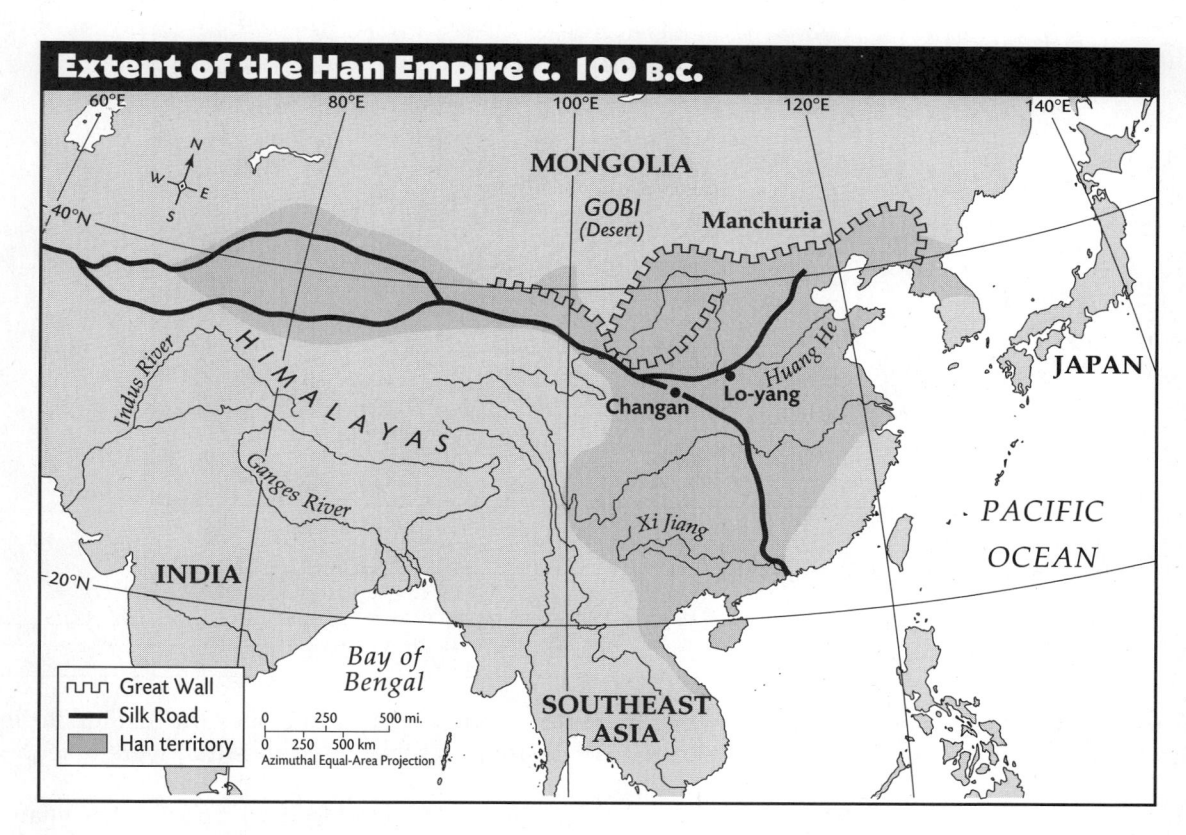

Extent of the Han Empire c. 100 B.C.

1. How far west from Changan did the Han Empire extend at its height? _____

2. Judging from what you know about China's geography, why do you think the Han Empire expanded only to the west? _____

3. Trace the paths of Han military campaigns under Wudi. Use arrows to show the advance of Wudi's troops into Southeast Asia, central Asia, and North Korea. Start your arrows from the center of the Han Empire. Label the Tarim Basin and the "Jade City" on the map. Remember that the "Jade City" marks the westernmost extent of the Great Wall. Finally, identify the area on your map that was controlled by the Hsiung-nu in northwestern Asia.

World History — Mapping History Activities

Name _____ Date _____ Class _____

MAPPING HISTORY Activity 10

Justinian's Conquests

After the Western Empire fell following several waves of invasions, Constantinople became the new power center for the empire. Byzantine emperor Justinian wanted to recover the lands lost to the invaders and reconstitute the Roman Empire. In the end, Justinian was able to take back much, but not all, of the territory that had once belonged to Rome. The map below shows Justinian's empire. Use it to complete the activities that follow.

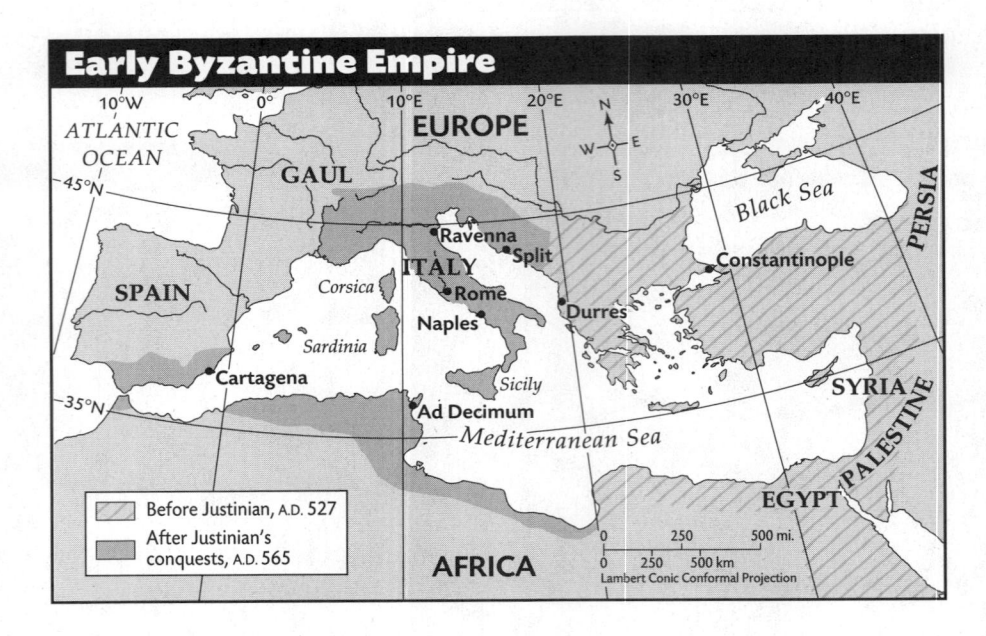

Early Byzantine Empire

Before Justinian, A.D. 527
After Justinian's conquests, A.D. 565

1. Constantinople is about how many miles from Rome? _____
2. Constantinople sits at the crossroads of which two bodies of water? _____
_____
3. Read the following historical description of Justinian's campaigns to take back the lost territories. Using the information provided, draw arrows on the map to show the routes that were taken.

In A.D. 533, the first expedition left Constantinople and was directed toward Africa. The Byzantine forces led by Belisarius landed in what is today the country of Tunisia. There, they defeated the Vandals in a battle at Ad Decimum and at the nearby city of Tricamarum. From there, the Byzantines sailed to Sicily, Sardinia, and Corsica and took back those islands. In A.D. 535, the second expedition was launched. This time, the plan was to recapture the Italian Peninsula. Belisarius, who occupied the island of Sicily, landed at Naples, fought his way to Rome, and pushed north to Ravenna. At the same time, Mundus, operating on the Balkan Peninsula, launched an invasion from Durres to Split. A third expedition was led by Liberius in A.D. 554. He landed at Cartagena and fought the Visigoths to take back Spain. Despite these successes, Justinian's expanded empire failed to include the interior of Gaul (now called France) or Spain.

10   Mapping History Activities   World History: The Human Experience

Name .... Date .... Class ....

MAPPING HISTORY Activity 11

Distant Outposts

During the period of Islamic civilization described in Chapter 11, the Islamic Empire had three different capitals. Madinah was the capital under the Rightly Guided Caliphs. The capital of the Umayyad dynasty was Damascus. The Abbasids built the city of Baghdad for their capital. The map below shows the Islamic Empire during four different periods. Use it to complete the activities that follow.

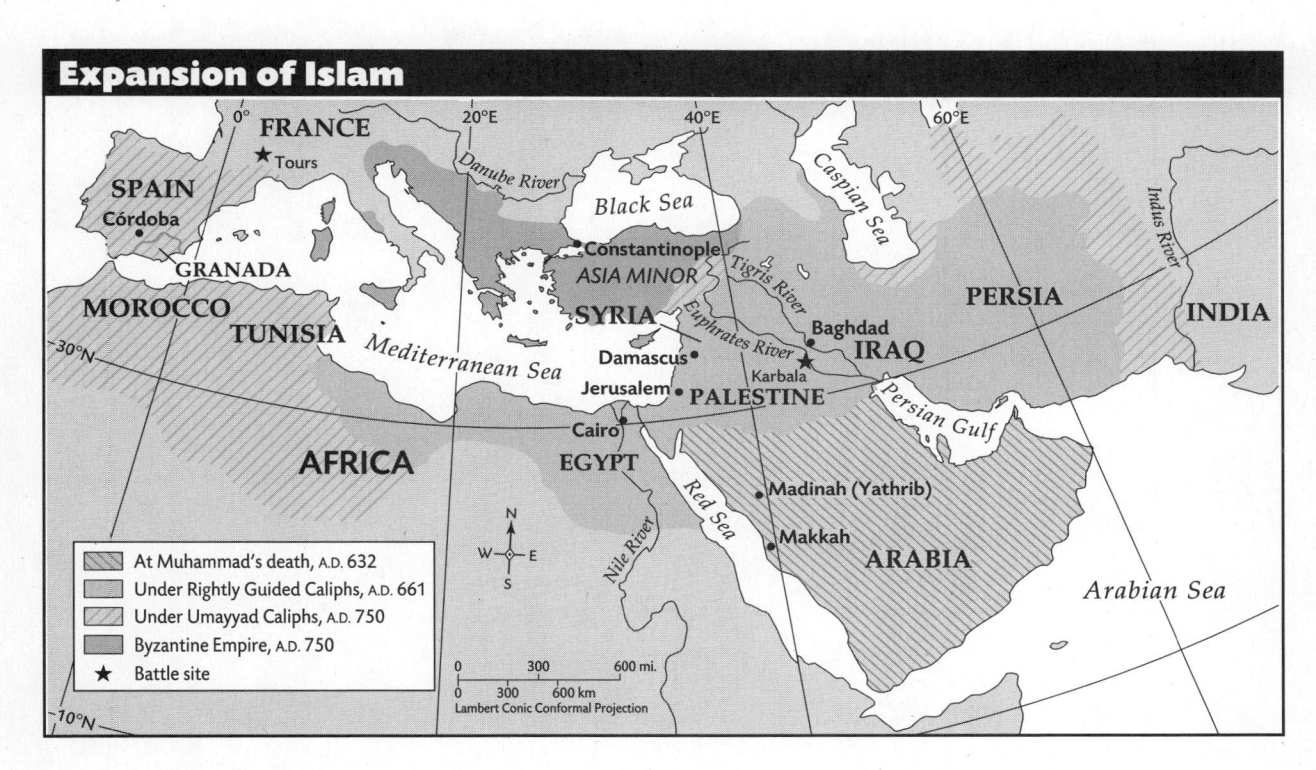

Expansion of Islam

Map showing the expansion of Islam with the following features:
- Locations labeled: FRANCE (Tours), SPAIN (Córdoba), GRANADA, MOROCCO, TUNISIA, AFRICA, EGYPT (Cairo), PALESTINE (Jerusalem), SYRIA (Damascus), ASIA MINOR (Constantinople), IRAQ (Baghdad, Karbala), PERSIA, INDIA, ARABIA (Madinah (Yathrib), Makkah)
- Bodies of water: Mediterranean Sea, Black Sea, Caspian Sea, Red Sea, Arabian Sea, Persian Gulf
- Rivers: Danube River, Tigris River, Euphrates River, Indus River, Nile River

Legend:
- At Muhammad's death, A.D. 632
- Under Rightly Guided Caliphs, A.D. 661
- Under Umayyad Caliphs, A.D. 750
- Byzantine Empire, A.D. 750
- ★ Battle site

Scale: 0–600 mi / 0–600 km
Lambert Conic Conformal Projection

1. What is the approximate distance from Makkah to Madinah? _____

2. How far is Madinah from Damascus? _____

3. What was the primary direction of Islamic expansion from the Arabian peninsula?
_____

4. In what direction would pilgrims traveling from Cairo to Makkah travel?
_____

5. The Muslim armies engaged in the jihad traveled along the North African coast to Morocco, then Spain, and north into France where their advance was stopped at the Battle of Tours. Draw the likely path followed by the armies.

6. What was the approximate distance traveled by Islamic armies from Makkah to Tours? _____

World History   Mapping History Activities   **11**

Name .... Date .... Class ....

MAPPING HISTORY Activity 12

The Walking Word

In A.D. 597, Pope Gregory I sent missionaries to England from Rome. Irish missionaries traveled overland from Ireland south and east, probably as far as Spain and Scandinavia. Partly due to the rule of Benedict and partly because of limited resources, many monks traveled on foot. Use the map below to complete the activities that follow. Use a separate sheet of paper.

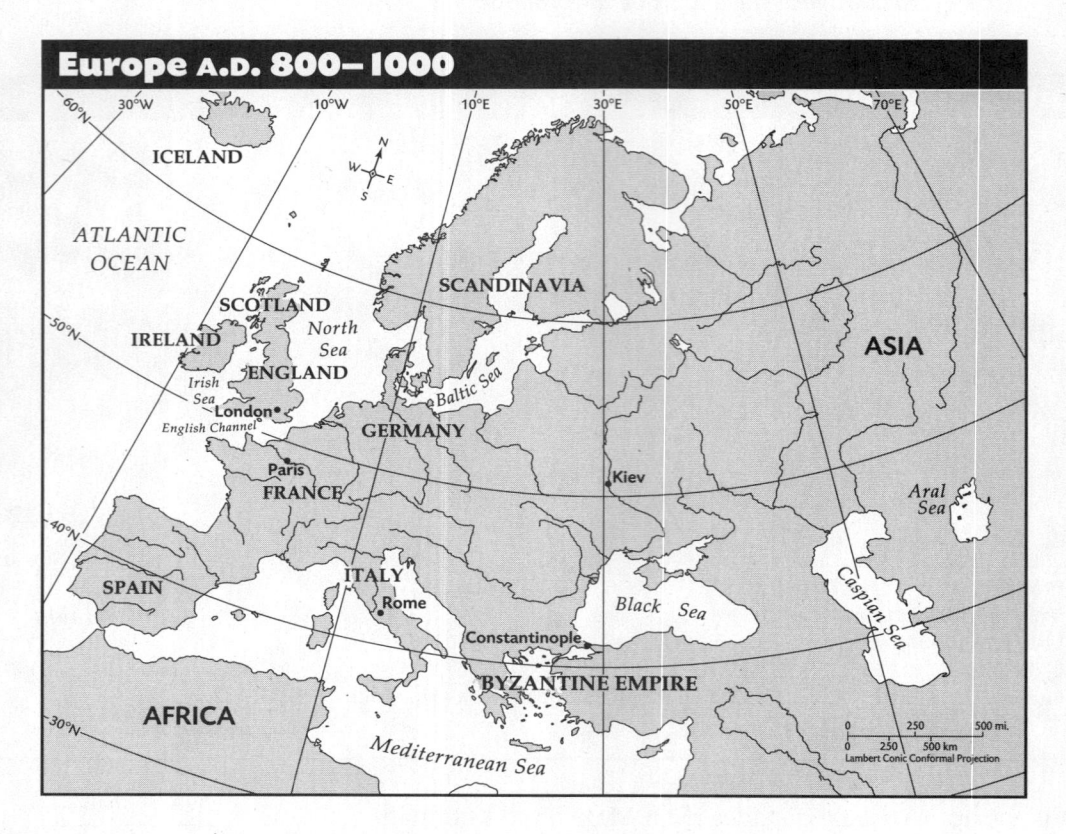

Europe A.D. 800–1000

1. What is the distance from Rome to London? From Ireland to Spain?
2. If a monk could walk 12 miles a day, how long would it take a missionary to reach London from Rome, adding a day for travel across the English Channel?
3. How long would it take a missionary to reach Spain from Ireland, via London and Paris, adding a day for travel across the Irish Sea and a day to cross the English Channel?
4. How long would it take a missionary to reach Scandinavia from Ireland, via London, France, and Germany, adding a day for travel across the English Channel, a day to cross the Irish Sea, and a day to cross the Baltic Sea?
5. Draw the three routes from Rome to Paris to London.

Name .... Date .... Class ....

MAPPING HISTORY Activity 13

France in A.D. 1400s

The Hundred Years' War between France and England lasted for 116 years. During this time, England had the advantage for the first 92 years, until the time of Joan of Arc. Having inspired the troops, Joan of Arc began driving the English back to the north of France. When the war ended in A.D. 1453, her efforts had helped push the English back to the port of Calais. The map below shows France in the A.D. 1400s. Use it to complete the activities that follow.

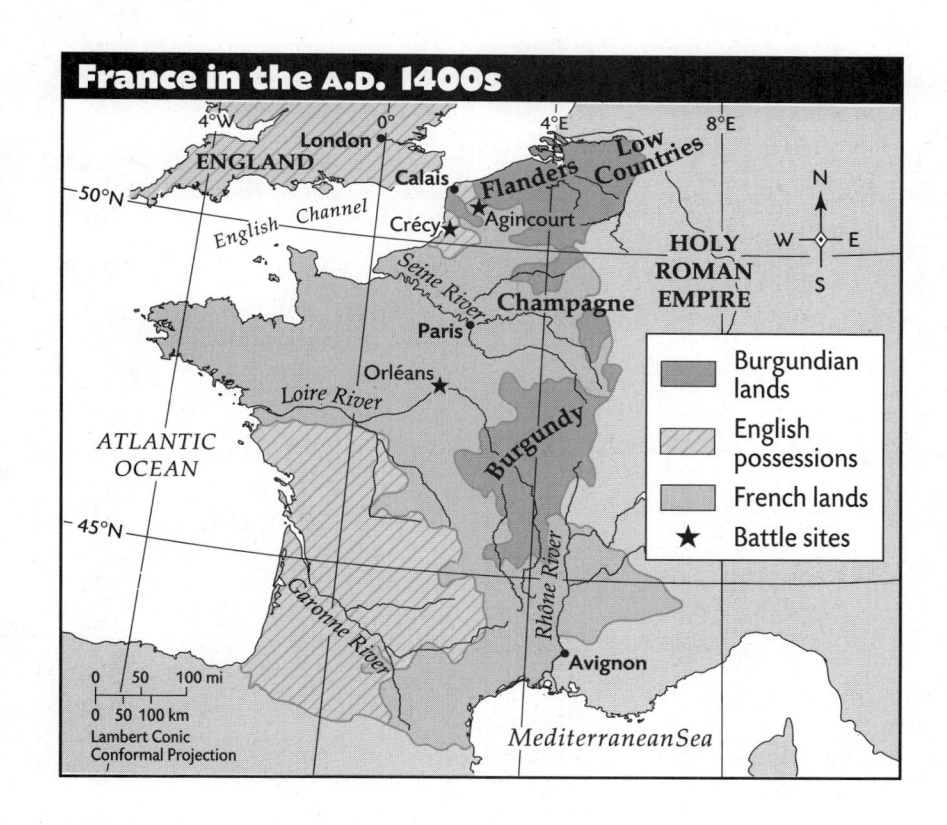

France in the A.D. 1400s

Map shows France with labeled features including: England, London, Calais, Crécy, Agincourt, Flanders, Low Countries, Holy Roman Empire, Champagne, Paris, Seine River, Orléans, Loire River, Burgundy, Rhône River, Atlantic Ocean, Garonne River, Avignon, Mediterranean Sea, English Channel. Legend: Burgundian lands, English possessions, French lands, Battle sites (★). Scale: 0–100 mi / 0–100 km. Lambert Conic Conformal Projection.

1. Which areas of France were occupied by English forces?

_____

2. Which areas of France were occupied by French forces?

_____

3. Name three cities that were strategic battle sites in the Hundred Years' War.

_____

4. Under Joan of Arc's leadership, the French battled from Orléans to Reims. Reims is approximately 80 miles (120 kilometers) northeast of Paris. Mark Reims on the map. Gradually, the French made their way to Calais. Trace the French forces' route from Orléans to Calais.

World History   Mapping History Activities   **13**

Name _____ Date _____ Class _____

MAPPING HISTORY Activity 14

Languages of East and Southeast Asia

Throughout East and Southeast Asia, hundreds of languages are spoken by diverse groups of people. Such diversity can often be confusing to historians seeking the origins of various ethnic groups. However, scientists known as linguists look for similarities in the grammar and vocabulary of different languages to see which ethnic groups are related. So far, linguists have identified at least five distinct language families, or languages that share similar structures and vocabulary, among Asian peoples. Observing how similar languages spread can give historians valuable insight into the interaction and movement of different ethnic groups. The map below shows East and Southeast Asia. Use it to complete the activities that follow.

1. Label the major Asian language families listed below on the corresponding areas of the map. Add a key to your map.

    Sinitic: China and most of Southeast Asia

    Altaic: Mongolia, Central Asia, Korea, Japan

    Austronesian: Malay and Indonesia

    Indo-European: India

    Khmer: Cambodia

2. Identify the language family spoken in each of the following cities.

    Borobudur _____

    Nara _____

3. There are more than 20,000 islands in the Philippine and Indonesian archipelagos. How do you think the Austronesian language might have spread through this area?

    _____

4. How might the spread of Islam by Arabians throughout central Asia and Indonesia have affected the languages spoken there? (Look back to Chapter 11 to review the language the Muslim people used.)

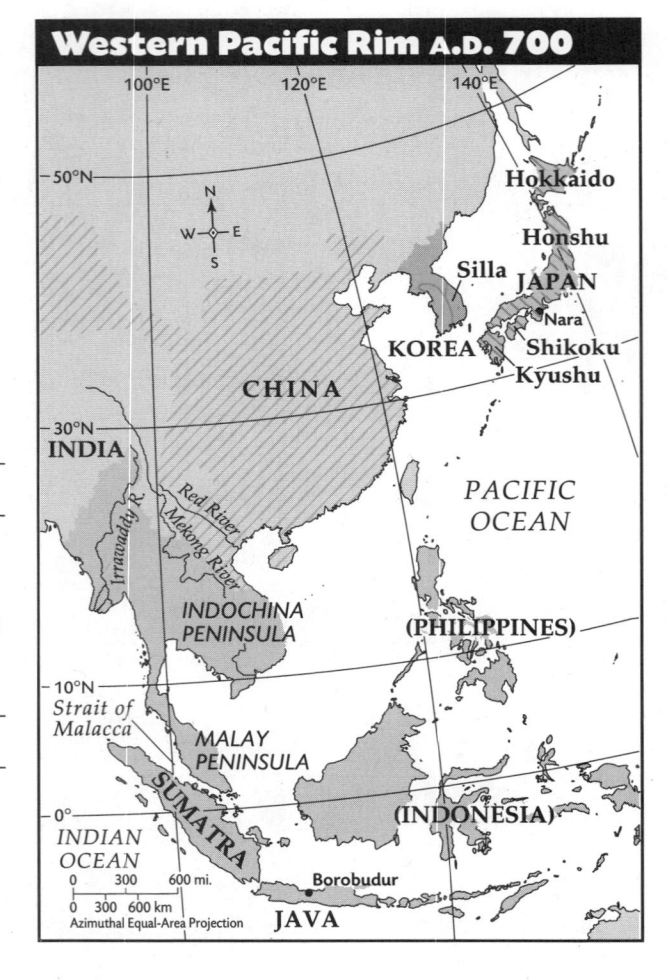

    _____
    _____
    _____

Western Pacific Rim A.D. 700

14   Mapping History Activities   World History

Name _____ Date _____ Class _____

MAPPING HISTORY Activity 15

Who Took What?

As European explorers arrived in the Americas, they took land from Native Americans and claimed it for their home countries. The map below shows the locations of Native American peoples before the arrival of Europeans. Use the map to complete the activities that follow.

Native American Cultures of North America

North American Peoples
- Arctic
- Subarctic
- Northwest Coast
- California–Great Basin
- Southwest
- Great Plains
- Eastern Woodlands

1. Choose three colors to represent the Spanish, English, and French holdings in North America. Add this information to the map key.

2. Use the following information to indicate on the map the lands held by Spain, England, and France:
   By the mid-A.D. 1600s, England controlled most of New England and all but the westernmost tip of Long Island, as well as the eastern shore of Chesapeake Bay. Spain had northern South America, Central America, Mexico, and the entire coast of Florida. France controlled the St. Lawrence River, Nova Scotia, Prince Edward Island, and the eastern portion of New Brunswick.

3. From which Native American peoples did the Spanish take land? _____

4. From which Native American peoples did the English take land? _____

5. From which Native American peoples did the French take land? _____

World History   Mapping History Activities   **15**

Name _____ Date _____ Class _____

MAPPING HISTORY Activity 16

The Success of Reform

The Protestant and Catholic Reformations during the Renaissance changed the face of religion in Europe. Instead of being almost exclusively Catholic, now Europe would be divided among several different religions: Catholic, Calvinist, Lutheran, Church of England, and others. Meanwhile, the Ottoman Empire in the east remained Orthodox whereas the majority of the eastern Mediterranean and North Africa remained Muslim. The map below shows the distribution of religions in Europe in 1560. Use it to complete the activities that follow.

Religions of Europe 1560

Dominant Religions: Roman Catholic, Calvinist, Lutheran, Church of England, Eastern Orthodox, Muslim

Minority Religions: A Anabaptist, C Calvinist, L Lutheran, RC Roman Catholic, O Eastern Orthodox, H Hussite, J Jewish

1. Approximately what percent of Europe north and west of the Ottoman Empire was Catholic? What percent was Protestant?

2. Look at the list of towns and cities in the chart. Locate each town or city on the map. Circle Protestant towns in blue and Catholic towns in red.

3. What does this tell you about how successful the Protestant and Catholic Reformations were?

Date	Event	Location
1517	Luther nails Ninety-five Theses on church door.	Wittenberg
1521	Luther rejects council's attempt to reclaim him.	Worms
1525	Huldrych Zwingli establishes theocracy.	Zurich
1541	John Calvin establishes Consistory.	Geneva
1534	Anabaptists seize control of city.	Münster
1542	Inquisition begins.	Rome
1545	Pope Paul III calls for Council to reform doctrine.	Trent

Name .... Date .... Class ....

MAPPING HISTORY Activity 17

Routes of Trade and Cultural Exchange

When the Europeans reached the Americas, native peoples living there already had their own well-established routes of trade and cultural exchange. The map below shows one such network of exchange centered around the cities of Teotihuacán and Tula. Use the map to complete the following activity.

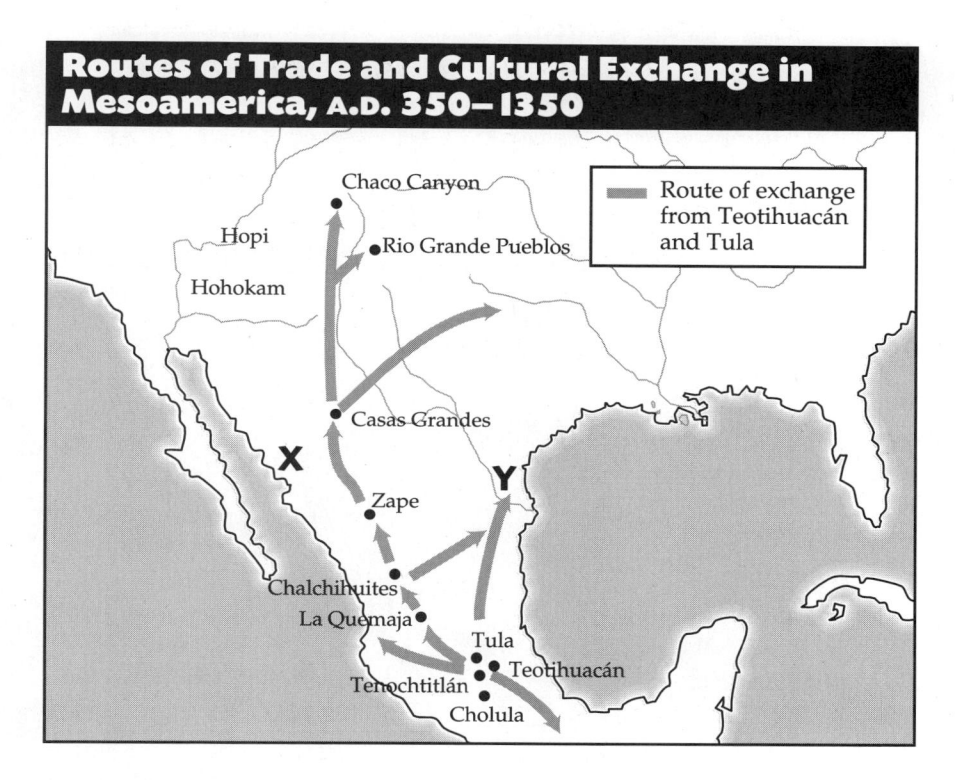

Routes of Trade and Cultural Exchange in Mesoamerica, A.D. 350–1350

— Route of exchange from Teotihuacán and Tula

Locations shown: Chaco Canyon, Hopi, Rio Grande Pueblos, Hohokam, Casas Grandes, X, Y, Zape, Chalchihuites, La Quemaja, Tula, Teotihuacán, Tenochtitlán, Cholula

1. How far north did the influence of the people of Teotihuacán and Tula extend?

    _____

2. Which trade route covers the greater distance, the route from Tula to Zape or the route from Zape to the Rio Grande Pueblos?

    _____

3. Using a different type of line or color, draw in the Cholula trade routes as described below. Be sure to add your line to the map key.

    The people of Cholula used the following routes of trade and cultural exchange:
    - northwest from Cholula along the west coast to the **X**
    - northeast from Cholula along the east coast to the **Y**
    - from Cholula to Casas Grandes to the Hohokam communities
    - from Cholula to Casas Grandes to the Hopi communities

World History   Mapping History Activities   **17**

Name .... Date .... Class ....

MAPPING HISTORY Activity 18

The Taiping Rebellion

The Taiping Rebellion in 1850 began in southern China under a mystical leader known as Hung Hsiu-ch'üan. Hung modeled himself as a revolutionary messiah [god on earth] by combining Christianity with his own unique theology. The map below shows the path of the Taiping army and the areas held by the Taipings. Use it to complete the activities that follow.

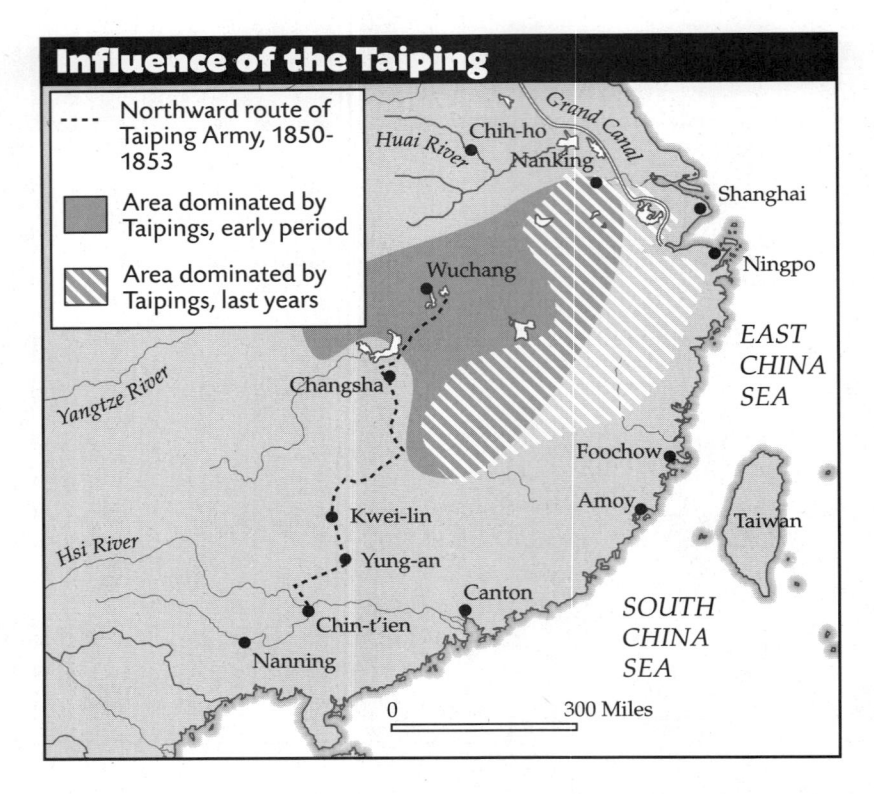

Influence of the Taiping

- - - - Northward route of Taiping Army, 1850-1853
▓ Area dominated by Taipings, early period
▨ Area dominated by Taipings, last years

0 ——— 300 Miles

1. What reasons might European countries have given to push for greater military power in China after the Taiping Rebellion?

_____

2. About how many miles long was the area dominated by Taipings in the early period?

_____

3. Given that Hung Hsiu-ch'üan came from southern China, where might he have gotten his first taste of Christian doctrine?

_____

4. This rebellion profoundly disturbed British foreigners in China working as traders in a system of ports along coastal and southern China from Canton to Shanghai. Using a marker or a colored pencil, shade the area occupied by the most Europeans in China.

Mapping History Activity 19

The Hapsburg Empire

The Hapsburgs reached their greatest power before the end of the 1500s: Charles V annexed Milan in 1535, Philip II conquered Portugal in 1580, and Spanish holdings in the Americas were expanding. However the Hapsburg power structure would collapse over the next decades. The map below shows the Hapsburg holdings in the mid-1500s. Use it to complete the activities that follow. Write your answers on a separate sheet of paper.

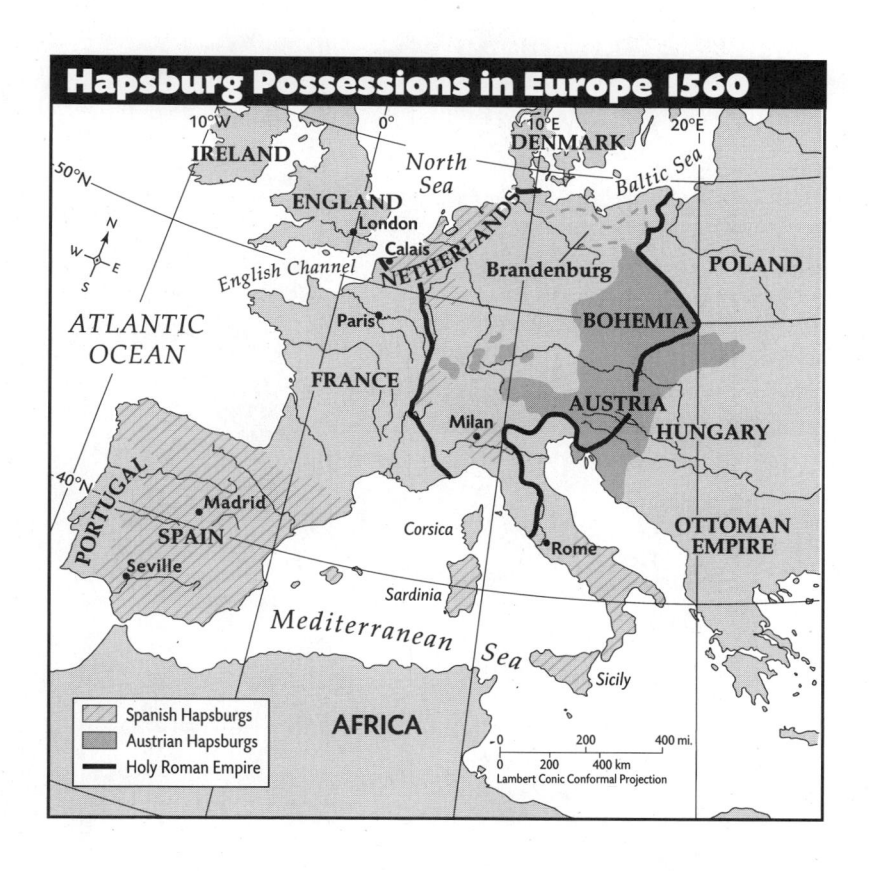

Hapsburg Possessions in Europe 1560

1. Based on the map, in what ways was the Hapsburg Empire powerful in the mid-1500s?

2. Did Philip II make a strategic error in locating the capital of the Spanish Hapsburg possessions in Madrid? Explain your answer.

3. Locate each of the lands held by the Spanish Hapsburgs. Based on the arrangement of countries, what location might have made a better capital than Madrid? Why?

4. The Spanish Armada suffered a disastrous defeat at the hands of the English. What other countries do you think Philip II could have had better success at conquering? Support your opinion with information from the map.

5. Use the Reference Atlas on page A12 to help you draw in the borders of the countries of present-day Europe. How has the configuration of the countries' borders changed in more than 400 years? How has it stayed the same?

Name _____ Date _____ Class _____

MAPPING HISTORY Activity 20

The Age of Revolution

Between 1500 and 1830, a revolution in scientific thinking spread across Europe. This scientific revolution affected politics, religion, philosophy, and the arts. The map below of present-day Europe shows places where significant developments in the scientific revolution and the Age of the Enlightenment occurred. Use the map to complete the activities that follow.

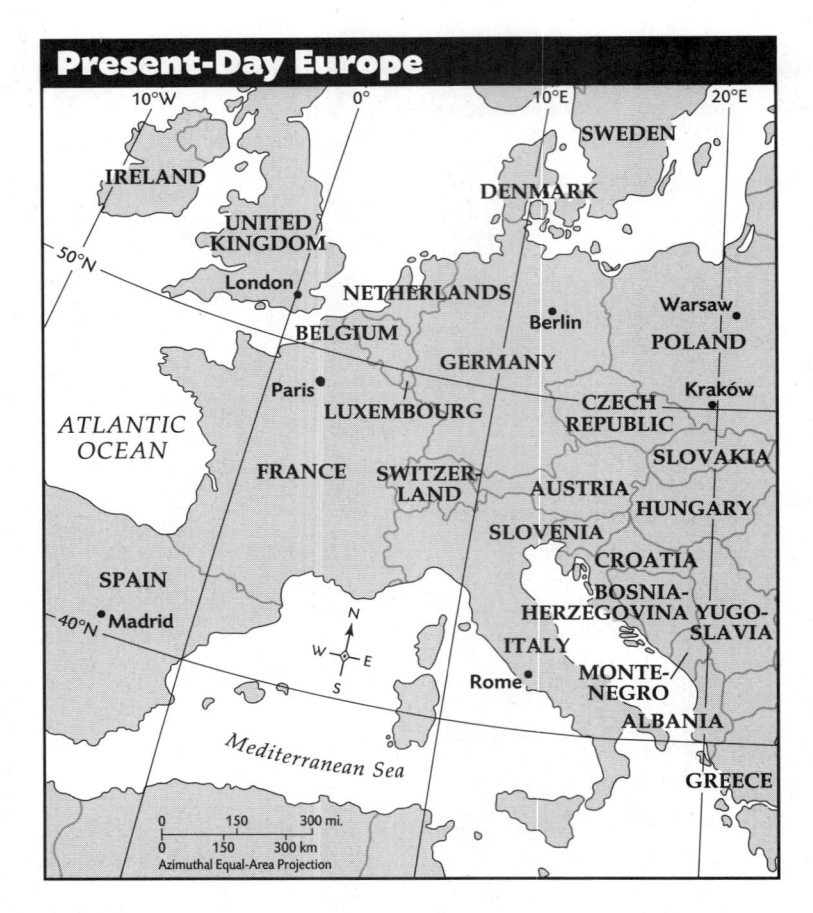

Present-Day Europe

1. Identify three nations shown on the map that did not exist in the Age of Enlightenment.

   _____

2. Identify three or more cities on the map that existed when the scientific revolution began, around 1500.

   _____

3. On the map, mark and label the city or country where the following developments in the scientific revolution and the Age of Enlightenment occurred: Copernicus begins his scientific career; Galileo stands trial for his heretical ideas; Charles II establishes the Royal Society; Madame de Pompadour draws together enlightened thinkers in salons; choosing exile from his native France over imprisonment, Voltaire begins a new phase of his career.

20   Mapping History Activities   World History

Name _____ Date _____ Class _____

MAPPING HISTORY Activity 21

Saratoga: Turning Point of the War for Independence

In 1777, the British formulated a plan to divide the colonies and win the war. The plan was to capture New York and cut off New England from the rest of the colonies. On paper, the plan was brilliant. In practice, however, the plan failed. The map below shows some early battles in the war. Use it to complete the activities that follow.

1. Use the information below to add dotted lines to the map showing the routes that were supposed to be followed by St. Leger and Howe. Add Burgoyne's route in a solid line.

   General John Burgoyne led an army that was to march down from Montreal to the Hudson River and follow the river valley south. Colonel Barry St. Leger was to sail down the St. Lawrence River to Lake Ontario, coming ashore near Oswego, then march to the Mohawk River, following it to meet other British forces. And General William Howe was to lead a force up the Hudson from New York City. What happened? St. Leger encountered resistance and was defeated at the Battle of Oriskany and turned back. Howe changed his mind and marched to Philadelphia instead, leaving Burgoyne alone. At Saratoga, in October 1777, outmaneuvered and outfought by colonial forces, Burgoyne surrendered his army of more than 5,000 men.

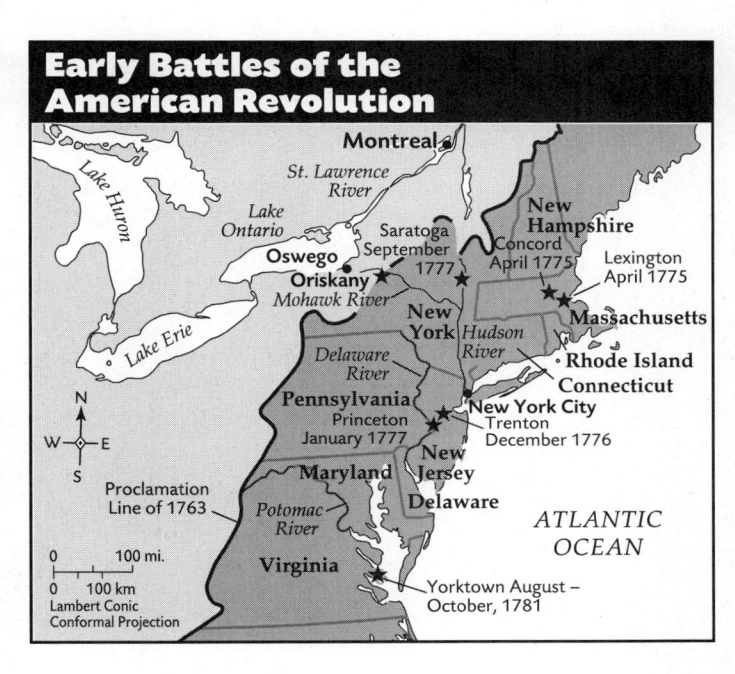

   Early Battles of the American Revolution

2. How far did Burgoyne's army travel from Montreal to Saratoga?

   _____

3. When he was defeated at the Battle of Oriskany, how far was St. Leger from Saratoga?

   _____

4. From the description of the planned routes each army was to take, identify which army had the easiest route and briefly explain why.

   _____

   _____

World History   Mapping History Activities   **21**

Name _____ Date _____ Class _____

MAPPING HISTORY Activity 22

The French Revolution

Napoleon so dominated Europe that the years 1800 to 1815 are often called "the Napoleonic Era." At the height of his power, Napoleon controlled virtually the entire continent. The map below illustrates the remarkable extent of his influence. Use it to complete the activities that follow. Write your answers on a separate sheet of paper.

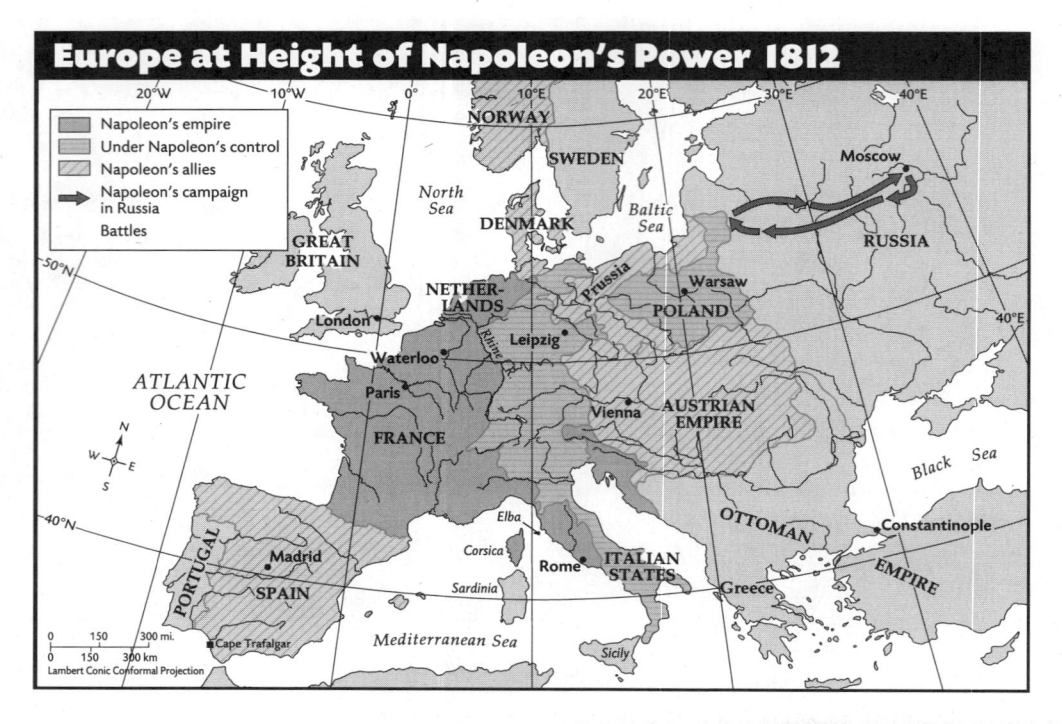

Europe at Height of Napoleon's Power 1812

Map legend:
- Napoleon's empire
- Under Napoleon's control
- Napoleon's allies
- Napoleon's campaign in Russia
- Battles

1. **a.** In what year was Napoleon at the height of his power?

   b. What nations did he control?

   c. What nations did he make his allies?

2. What parts of Europe did he fail to conquer?

3. Napoleon's major battles are listed in the chart at right.

   a. Create a map symbol for a battle and add the symbol to the map key.

   b. Using the symbol you created, mark the location of each battle on the map. Write the date of each battle next to its symbol.

   c. One historian said that between 1800 and 1815 "warfare ravaged Europe." Study the map. Do you agree? Explain your answer.

Battle	Date	Approximate Location
Marengo	1800	300 miles northwest of Rome
Trafalgar	1805	off the coast of Cape Trafalgar
Austerlitz	1805	250 miles southwest of Warsaw
Auerstedt	1806	just southwest of Leipzig
Jena	1806	just southeast of Auerstedt
Friedland	1807	extreme northern Poland, about 100 miles from the Baltic Sea
Peninsular War	1808–1814	throughout Spain
Wagram	1809	just north of Vienna
Aspern	1809	just northeast of Vienna
Borodino	1812	about 100 miles west of Moscow
Lützen	1813	about 100 miles west of Leipzig
Leipzig	1813	at Leipzig
Ligny	1815	about 100 miles southeast of Waterloo
Waterloo	1815	at Waterloo

Name _____ Date _____ Class _____

MAPPING HISTORY Activity 23

The Domestic System and Water Transportation

As you read in Section 1, the domestic system originated in Great Britain's woolen industry in the 1700s. This system also played a role in other industries—notably coal production and metal goods production. Rivers and canals provided people with an interconnected water system on which to transport the raw materials and finished goods of England's early industries. Use the map below to answer the questions and complete the activity.

English Industrial Areas and Waterways, c. 1750

Map shows: SCOTLAND, Newcastle, North Sea, Irish Sea, Ouse, Leeds, Humber, Manchester, Liverpool, Sheffield, Witham, Trent, Birmingham, Nene, Norwich, WALES, Severn, Avon, Bath, London, Thames, Exeter, English Channel.

Legend:
- Major areas of woolen cloth production
- Major areas of metal goods production
- Coal-producing areas
- Navigable rivers
- Canals built between 1760 and 1800

Scale: 0–100 mi / 0–150 km

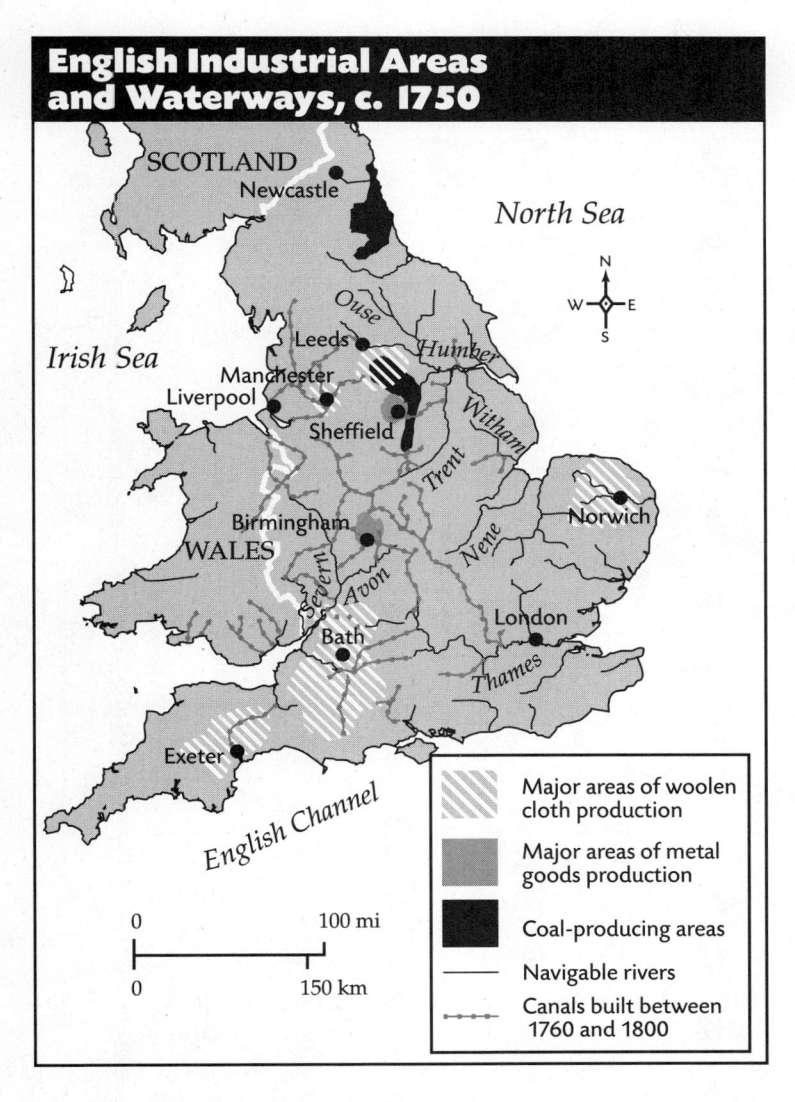

1. Which English cities were located in major areas of woolen cloth production?
   _____
   _____
   _____

2. Where were the major areas of coal production located?
   _____
   _____
   _____

3. What kind of waterway connected Leeds and Liverpool?
   _____
   _____
   _____

4. Which waterway would have been used to transport metal goods from Sheffield to the North Sea for export?
   _____
   _____
   _____

5. Assuming that it was easier and less expensive to transport goods by water than over land, what would have been the best routes to take when moving goods from Bath to London and from Birmingham to London? On the map, indicate the routes you would use.

World History   Mapping History Activities   23

Name _____ Date _____ Class _____

MAPPING HISTORY Activity 24

The Voyage of the *Beagle*

When Charles Darwin left England on the *Beagle* in 1831, he expected to be gone for two years. Instead, his voyage took five years. H.M.S. *Beagle* was a surveying vessel for the British Navy. Darwin had been hired to be the ship's naturalist, and at each stop on the voyage, he collected all kinds of specimens, many of which he dissected or stuffed. He took numerous notes on his observations.

The most important—and famous—stop on his trip was the visit to the Galápagos Islands. The observations he made there would later launch his theory of evolution. Use the map below to complete the activities that follow.

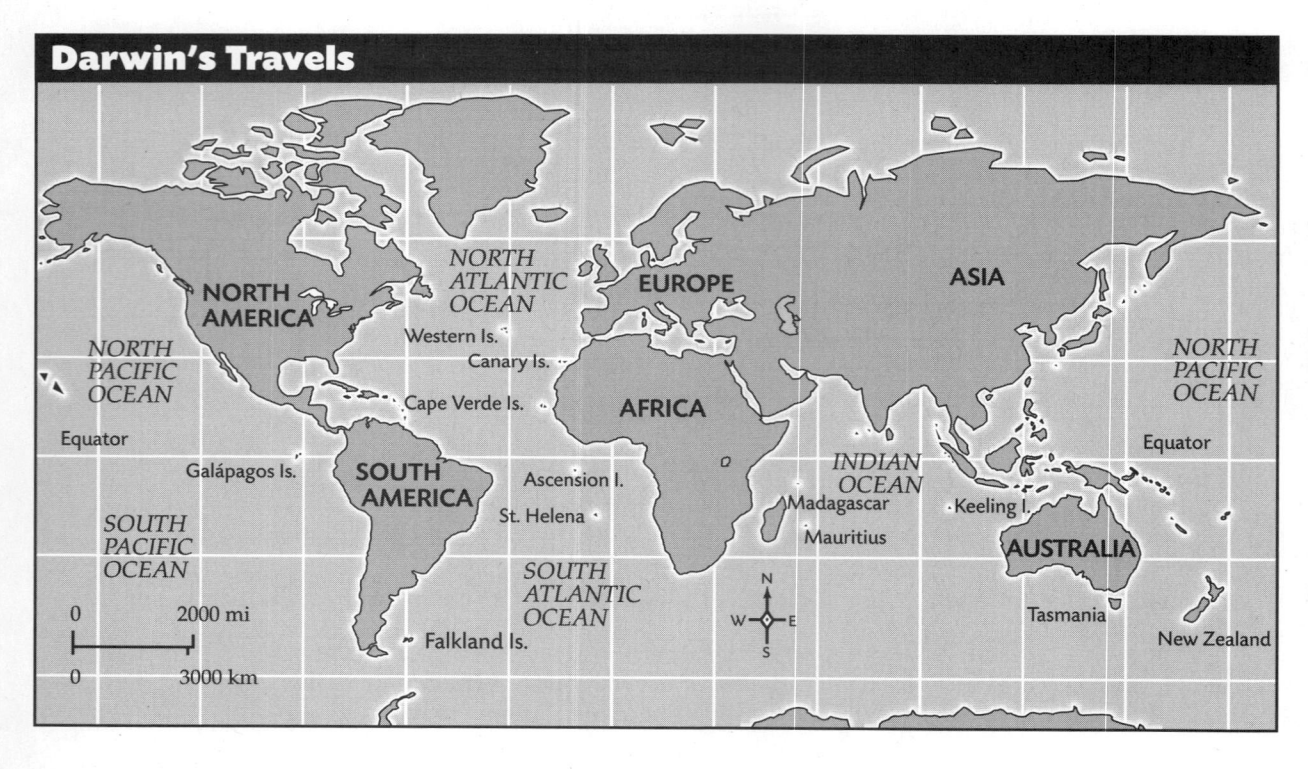

Darwin's Travels

1. Use the map scale to estimate the distance of the Galápagos Islands from the mainland. _____

2. Using the information below, plot the course the *Beagle* followed on the map above.

   After leaving England, the *Beagle* traveled first to the Canary Islands, then to the Cape Verde Islands, and on to the east coast of South America. It traveled around Cape Horn, up the west coast of South America, and out to the Galápagos Islands. From there it traveled west to New Zealand and Australia, through the Indian Ocean, and around the Cape of Good Hope to Ascension Island. It then headed back to Cape Verde, the Western Isles, and home.

Mapping History Activities   World History

Name .... Date .... Class ....

MAPPING HISTORY Activity 25

The Expanding United States

During the 1800s, the United States expanded several times. Some lands were purchased and others were acquired through treaties. The map below shows several additions to the United States. Create a map key to show which territories the United States acquired in each decade. Select a distinct color or pattern for each time period indicated and use the information contained in your textbook to recode the map below. Then answer the questions that follow.

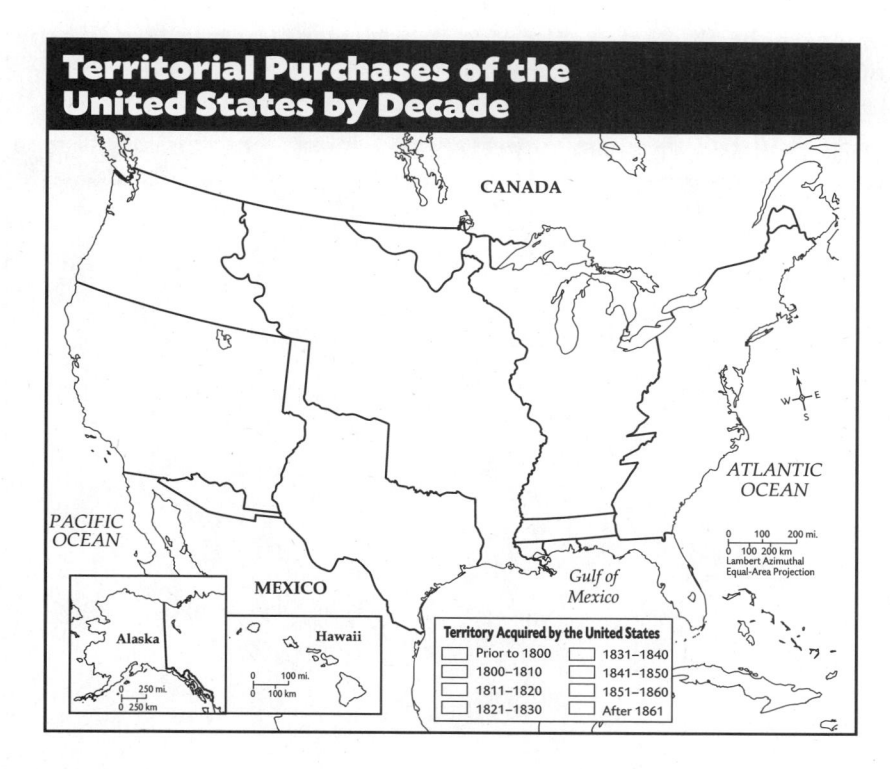

Territorial Purchases of the United States by Decade

Territory Acquired by the United States
- Prior to 1800
- 1800–1810
- 1811–1820
- 1821–1830
- 1831–1840
- 1841–1850
- 1851–1860
- After 1861

1. During which two decades was most of the territory of the United States acquired?

2. In which of the decades shown on the key did the United States NOT acquire territory?

3. How did the land the United States acquired after 1860 differ from previous acquisitions?

4. Compare the map on page 664 in your textbook with the map you have completed. How are they similar? How are they different?

World History   Mapping History Activities   **25**

Name .... Date .... Class ....

MAPPING HISTORY Activity 26

The Economy of Austria-Hungary

The *Ausgleich*, or Compromise, of 1867 restored Hungary's independence and established a dual monarchy within Austria-Hungary. The two states were politically independent, but they depended on each other economically. Industrialized Austria provided manufactured goods, while agricultural Hungary provided food products. This was an arrangement that satisfied the Austrian-Germans and Hungarian Magyars, who held power in the two states. Three-fifths of the population of the empire were Slavs, however, and they had no voice in the government. The map below shows the locations of the different peoples of Austria-Hungary. Use it to complete the activities that follow.

Peoples of Austria-Hungary 1914

1. Where did most of the Germans in Austria-Hungary live? _____

2. In which of the cities shown on the map would a Slavic person be most likely to live?
_____

3. After the creation of the dual monarchy, Bohemia and Moravia became leading producers of machine tools, textiles, armaments, shoes, and chemicals while Hungary remained agricultural, providing food products such as corn, wheat, and cattle. Create symbols for these products, then add them to the appropriate areas of the map key and your map.

26   Mapping History Activities   World History

Name .... Date .... Class ....

MAPPING HISTORY Activity 27

Africa's Natural Resources

Many European nations sought to control the diverse natural resources of Africa. The map below shows political boundaries in Africa in 1914. The table lists the location of many of Africa's resources. Regions with large deposits are shown in dark type. First, create symbols to complete the key and indicate on the map how natural resources were dispersed across the African continent. Then answer the questions that follow.

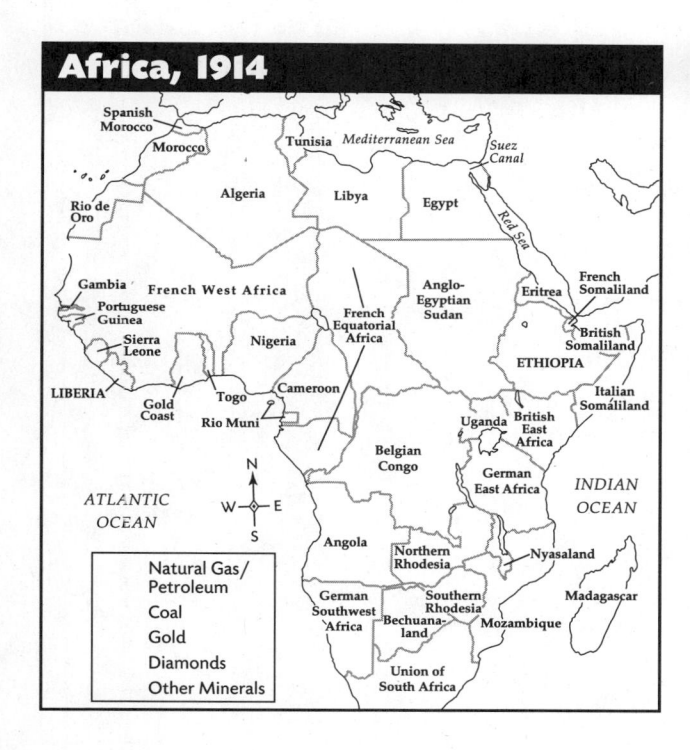

Africa, 1914

Resource	Location
Petroleum and Natural Gas	**Algeria, Libya,** Egypt, **Nigeria,** Angola, French Equatorial Africa (coastal region)
Coal	**Union of South Africa**
Gold	Gold Coast, Belgian Congo, **Union of South Africa**
Diamonds	Sierra Leone, German East Africa, Angola, **Union of South Africa, Belgian Congo,** Bechuanaland
Other Minerals	Morocco (lead), Gold Coast (bauxite), **Northern Rhodesia** (copper, uranium), Southern Rhodesia (copper), French West Africa (uranium), German Southwest Africa (zinc, uranium)

1. In which regions of Africa is most of the continent's petroleum and natural gas found?

   _____

2. Which resources would have been found in the British colonies south of the Equator?

   _____

3. Look at the map on page 710 in your textbook and review the landholdings of European nations in Africa. Compare the territory claimed by France, Portugal, Great Britain, and Germany. Then rank the countries from 1 to 4 on the basis of the natural resources they controlled. Give your reasons for each ranking.

   Most Control of Resources   1. _____

   2. _____

   3. _____

   Least Control of Resources   4. _____

World History   Mapping History Activities   **27**

Name .... Date .... Class ....

MAPPING HISTORY Activity 28

World War I in the Balkans

When fighting broke out in Europe in 1914, the Allies and the Central Powers fought for control of the Balkan Peninsula and the Ottoman Empire. The map below shows these areas. Use it to complete the activities that follow. Write your answers on a separate sheet of paper.

1. Which countries in the Balkan Peninsula sided with the Allies?

2. Why was it important for the Allies to attempt the Gallipoli invasion?

3. Why did it make sense for both Austria-Hungary and Bulgaria to attempt an attack on Romania?

4. Read the following passage, then follow the instructions below.
The Central Powers led an offensive against Serbia in 1915. Attacks were launched from Austria-Hungary just north of Belgrade and from Sofia. The armies came together west of Skopje near the Albanian border. Another attack came from Sarajevo and pushed south into Albania. In 1916 the German forces that had succeeded in moving the Eastern Front into Russia turned south to conquer Romania. Falkenhayn led an offensive from several points in southeastern Austria-Hungary toward the capital city of Bucharest and the Black Sea port of Constanz. Mackensen led forces from northeastern Bulgaria to these same cities. All of the territory north of the line running from Valona to Salonika fell into Central Powers' hands. The Allies finally were able to counterattack. In 1918 they moved in from Greek territory. The French and British troops arrived at the port of Salonika. From there, they drove north through Serbia to Belgrade and from there to Budapest. The Central Powers were unable to halt the advances of the Allied troops. Other regiments battled on to Sofia and to Constantinople in order to end the Central Powers' dominance over the peninsula.

    a. Using red markers, draw arrows to show the movements of the Central Powers' troops.

    b. Shade in the territory conquered by the Central Powers.

    c. Using blue markers, draw in the counteroffensive staged by the Allies in 1918 to win back the Balkan Peninsula.

Balkan Peninsula and Surrounding Regions

Mapping History Activities

World History

Name .... Date .... Class ....

MAPPING HISTORY Activity 29

Movements of People 1919–1939

After World War I, the map of Europe changed. Although efforts were made to draw new boundaries on the basis of self-determination of ethnic groups, not every minority group became a separate nation. Some minority ethnic groups remained within the boundaries of other groups. Throughout the period between the two world wars, many minority ethnic groups left their homes to escape persecution and violence. Others emigrated because their government forced them to do so.

The map below shows Europe in the 1930s. Read the following statements describing the movements of various minority ethnic groups during the 1919–1939 period. Draw arrows on the map to represent the movements described. Use a different color for each ethnic group and add a key to show the meaning of each color.

European Borders, 1930s

1. Following an agreement at the end of the Greek-Turkish war, Greece and Turkey exchanged their minority populations. About 400,000 Turks from northeastern Greece were moved to Turkey, while 1,250,000 Greeks were sent to Greece from Turkey in 1924.
2. Between 1919 and 1939, Turkey also received 80,000 Turks from Romania; 110,000 Turks from Bulgaria; and around 20,000 Turks from Yugoslavia.
3. As a result of the Treaty of Versailles, many Germans moved back to Germany: 350,000 from the north of newly constituted Poland; 90,000 from the south of Poland; 40,000 from western Czechoslovakia; and 120,000 from the northeastern corner of France.
4. About 290,000 Jews and other refugees from the Nazi regime migrated either overseas, or to Belgium, the Netherlands, France, and Switzerland.
5. Hungary received 200,000 ethnic Hungarians from Romania; 80,000 from northern Yugoslavia; and 120,000 from eastern Czechoslovakia.

World History — Mapping History Activities

Name .... Date .... Class ....

MAPPING HISTORY Activity 30

The Long March

In 1934, nearly surrounded by the Guomindang forces, Mao Zedong led the Red Army in a retreat covering about 6,000 miles (9,600 kilometers) and lasting one year. The army marched into some of the most remote regions of China, defeating ten provincial armies while being chased by the Guomindang. Now known as the Long March, this desperate bid for survival killed tens of thousands of soldiers. Using the information given below, trace the approximate route of the Long March on the map of China. Then answer the questions that follow.

The Long March began in Yudu, in the southwestern corner of Jiangxi province, and continued southwest to Chenxian in Hunan province. From there the march continued west and slightly north to the area around Zunyi, where the army crossed mountains. From Zunyi, the Red Army traveled west and south to just north of Kunming in Yunnan province.

Somewhat west of Kunming, the Long March headed north. The northward course continued for about 500 miles (800 kilometers). Then the march took a gradual northeastern direction to pass slightly east and south of Lanzhou. From there the march continued north and east, staying east of the Huang He, and ended at Wuqi.

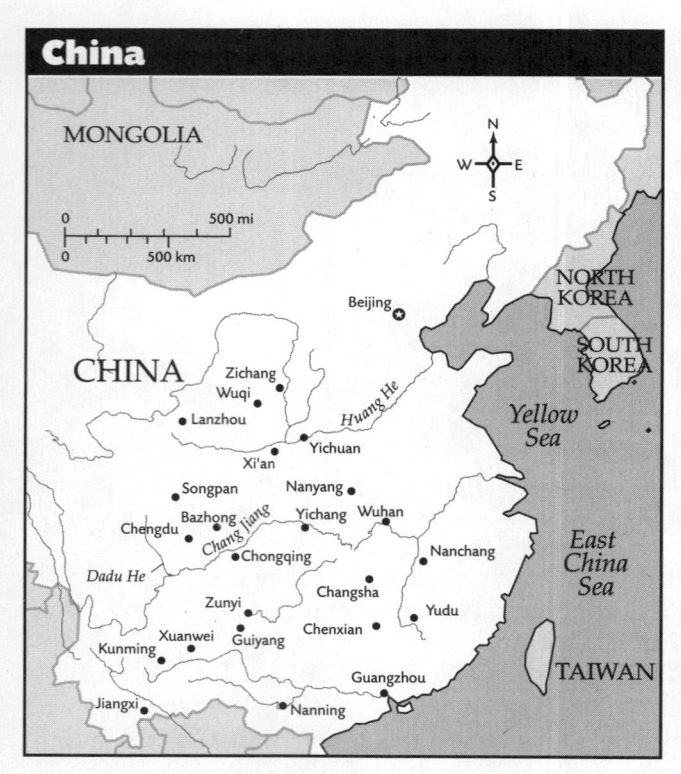

China

[Map of China showing Mongolia, North Korea, South Korea, Taiwan, Yellow Sea, East China Sea, and cities including Beijing, Zichang, Wuqi, Lanzhou, Xi'an, Yichuan, Songpan, Nanyang, Bazhong, Yichang, Wuhan, Chengdu, Chongqing, Nanchang, Dadu He, Changsha, Zunyi, Yudu, Xuanwei, Chenxian, Kunming, Guiyang, Guangzhou, Jiangxi, Nanning. Rivers shown: Huang He, Chang Jiang.]

1. Compare this map to the one on pages A16–A17 of your textbook. What sort of terrain did the long march cover?
   _____
   _____

2. About how far, "as the crow flies," did the Red Army end up from the starting point on the march? _____

3. Near Zunyi, the path of the Long March made many turns and doubled back on itself. What might have been the cause of these movements?
   _____
   _____
   _____
   _____
   _____

Name _____ Date _____ Class _____

MAPPING HISTORY Activity 31

War on a Global Scale

One of the main arguments used by the Axis powers to support their imperialist conquests was the need for raw materials and food. The wheat fields of the Soviet Union and its oil resources became primary targets for German forces. Likewise, Japan targeted the tin, rubber, and oil of Southeast Asia held by France and Great Britain. The map below shows areas affected by World War II. Use it to complete the activities that follow.

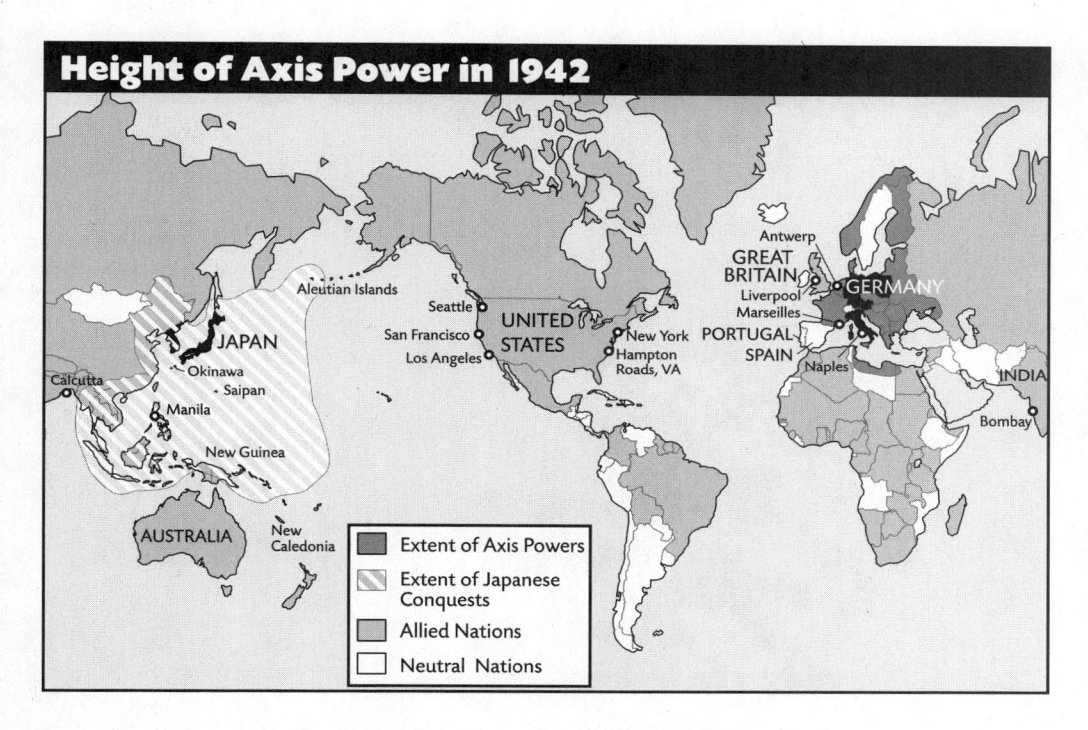

Height of Axis Power in 1942

- Extent of Axis Powers
- Extent of Japanese Conquests
- Allied Nations
- Neutral Nations

1. What prevented Germany from controlling all of continental Europe?

_____

2. The Japanese and the Germans both controlled areas bordering on which country?

_____

3. Read the following description of how the United States Army was able to supply the war effort on both fronts. Then draw the supply lines that are described.

   From New York, the United States Army sent supplies to the port cities of Liverpool, England; Antwerp, Belgium; Marseilles, France; and Naples, Italy. Supplies from Hampton Roads, Virginia, were shipped all the way to Bombay, India. On the Pacific side, the United States supplied the Aleutian Islands of Alaska from Seattle. As the United States advanced on Japanese possessions in this region, it shipped supplies from San Francisco to New Caledonia, the eastern coast of Australia, the island of New Guinea, the island of Saipan, Manila in the Philippines, and Okinawa (after conquest by the Allied forces). From Los Angeles, supplies were sent all the way to Calcutta, India, allowing the Allies to push back the Japanese from the west.

World History   Mapping History Activities   **31**

Name _____ Date _____ Class _____

MAPPING HISTORY Activity 32

Europe Divided

After World War II, Europe was divided into Soviet and Western spheres of influence. The map below shows Europe from 1945 to 1955. Use it to complete the following activity.

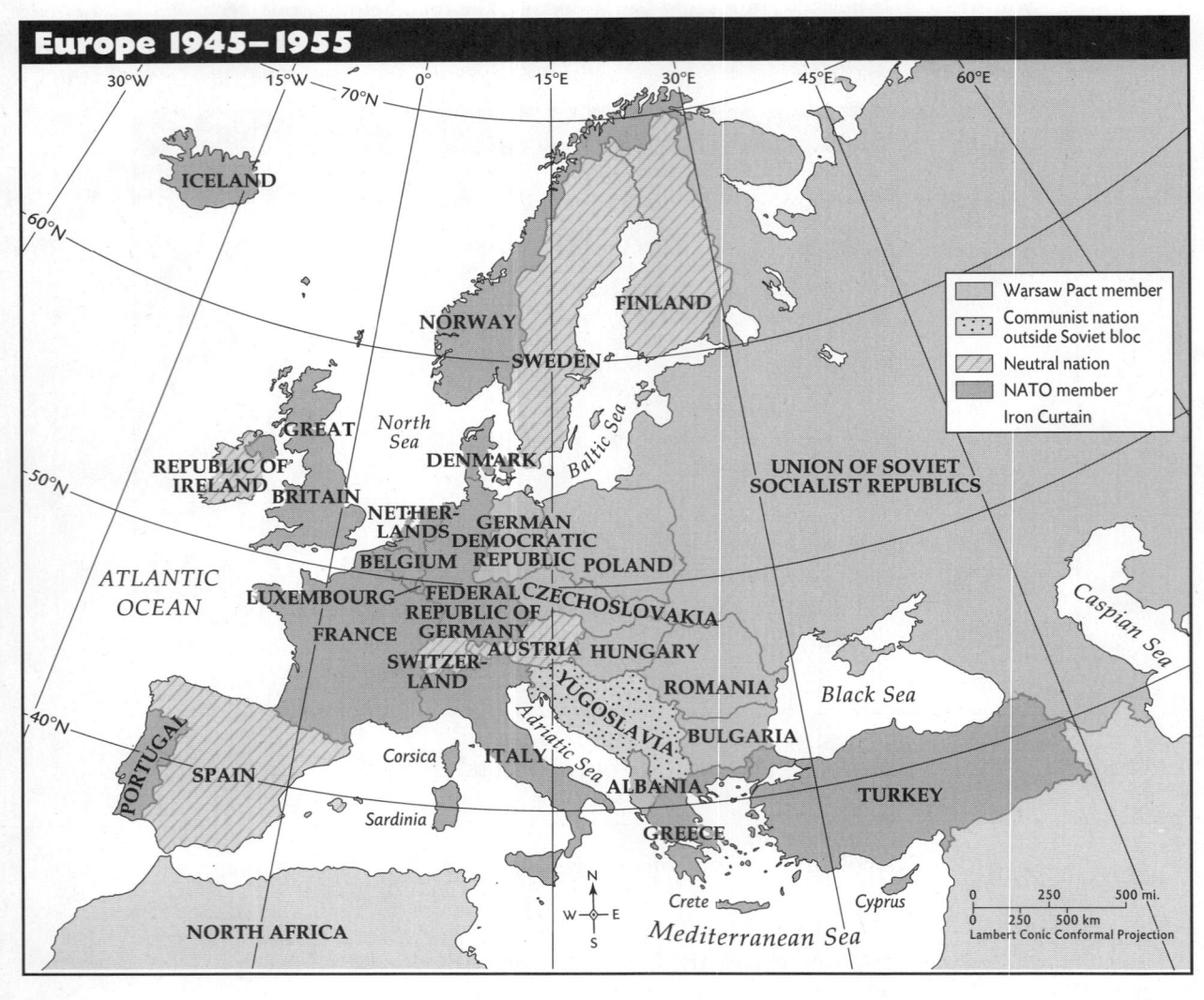

Europe 1945–1955

Map legend:
- Warsaw Pact member
- Communist nation outside Soviet bloc
- Neutral nation
- NATO member
- Iron Curtain

1. During the cold war, most European nations aligned themselves with the Soviet Union or the United States; however, Finland and Austria remained neutral. Describe the location of these two nations relative to Warsaw Pact members and then formulate a hypothesis to explain Finland's and Austria's neutrality.

2. In 1946 Winston Churchill observed that "from Stettin in the Baltic to Trieste in the Adriatic an iron curtain has descended across the continent of Europe." Using a colored pencil, revise the map to show the iron curtain that Churchill described. Add the iron curtain to the map key.

Name .... Date .... Class ....

MAPPING HISTORY Activity 33

Agriculture in China

With nearly 20 percent of the world's population living within its borders, the production of crops and textiles poses a distinct problem for modern China. The map below charts the major zones of cultivation in China and shows where individual crops are produced. Look at the map and then complete the activities that follow.

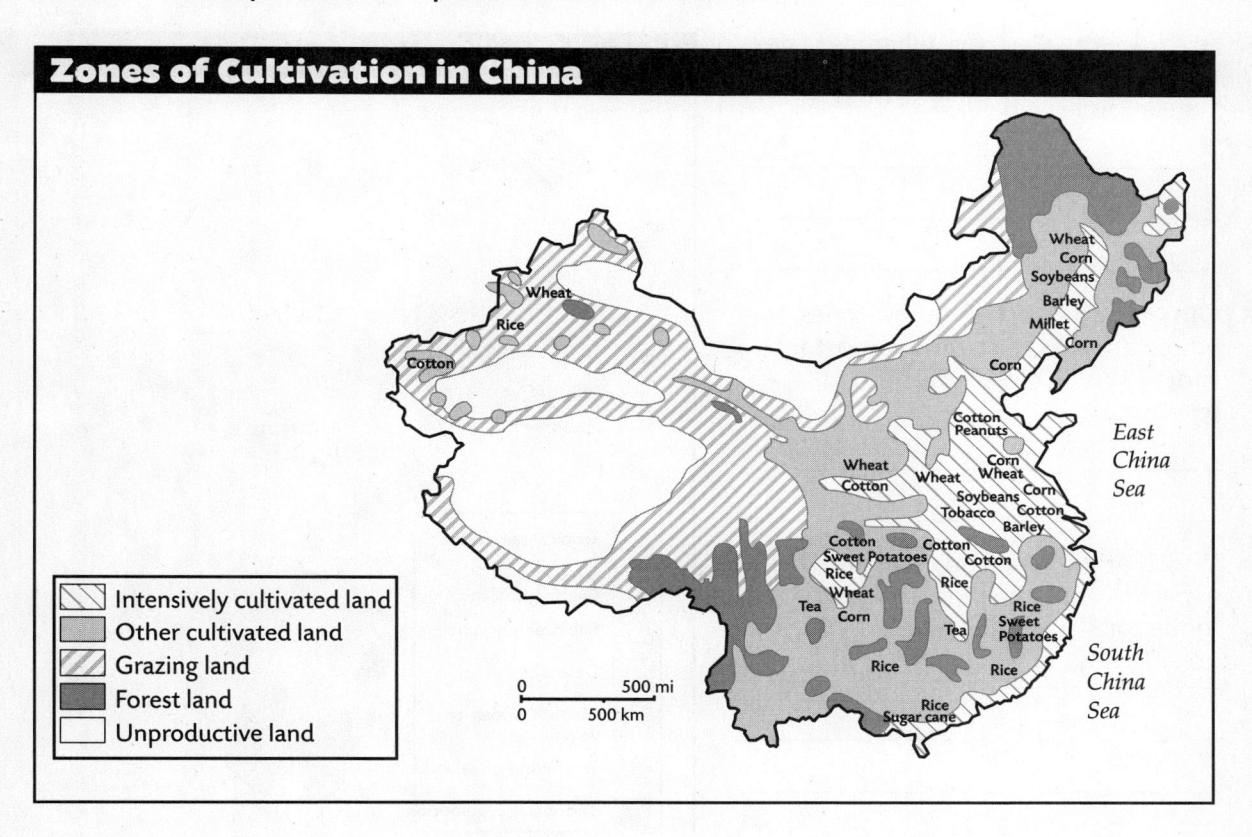

Zones of Cultivation in China

Key:
- Intensively cultivated land
- Other cultivated land
- Grazing land
- Forest land
- Unproductive land

1. Which area or areas of China produce most of the crops for human consumption? Shade this area on the map and add a key explaining your markings.

2. In what region(s) of China would you most expect to find farmers raising cattle and other domesticated animals? Shade this area on the map and add a key explaining your markings. Then explain your reasoning below.

   _____

   _____

3. How does a map that labels specific products differ from one that simply indicates agricultural areas?

   _____

   _____

World History   Mapping History Activities   33

Name .... Date .... Class ....

MAPPING HISTORY Activity 34

African Vegetation

Africa is a huge continent—the second largest on the earth. Across its vast lands, vegetation varies dramatically as a result of differences in climates, soil quality, and many other factors. The map below shows vegetation zones of Africa. Use it to complete the activities that follow.

1. According to the map, where is vegetation most dense in Africa? Where is vegetation least dense?

   _____
   _____
   _____

2. Out of the seven vegetation zones, which appears to cover the most territory? Which covers the least territory?

   _____
   _____

3. Which of the seven areas would you expect to have the highest yield of food crops? Explain.

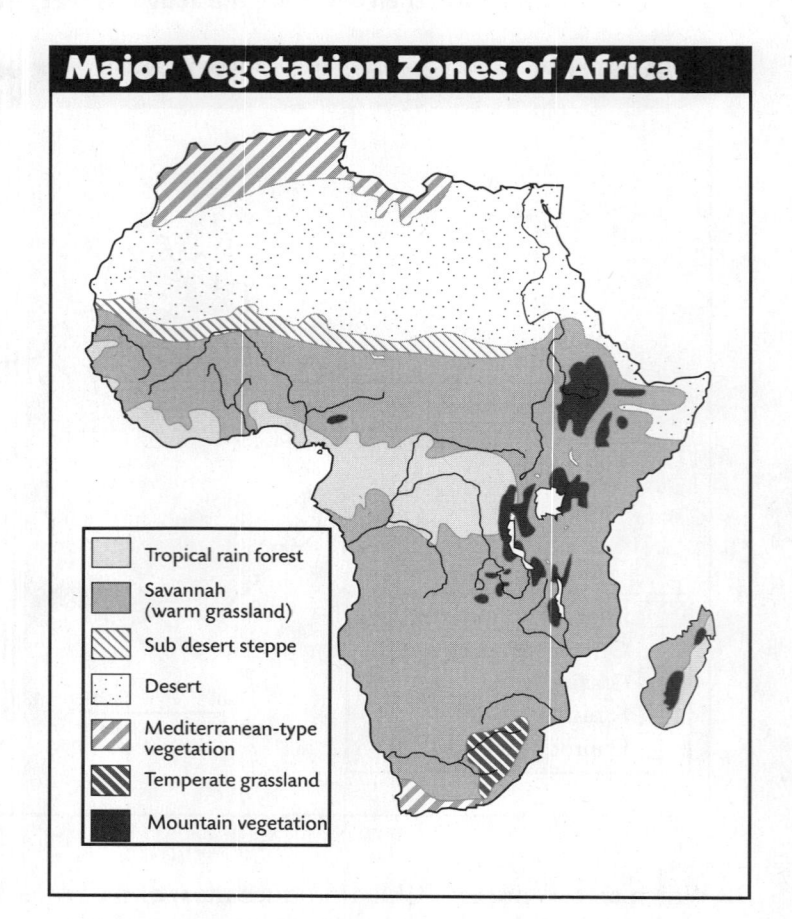

   _____
   _____
   _____
   _____

Major Vegetation Zones of Africa

Legend:
- Tropical rain forest
- Savannah (warm grassland)
- Sub desert steppe
- Desert
- Mediterranean-type vegetation
- Temperate grassland
- Mountain vegetation

4. Refer to the map on page 947 of your textbook. Use a colored pencil to mark on the map above the areas that are heavily populated (greater than 60 people per square mile).

5. What relationships do you see between vegetation and population density?

   _____
   _____

6. What other factors besides vegetation may influence where a person lives?

   _____
   _____

34   Mapping History Activities   World History

Name _____ Date _____ Class _____

MAPPING HISTORY Activity 35

Who's Got the Oil?

Oil is the most important natural resource of the Middle East. The value of oil is one of the reasons that the United States, the major European powers, and other countries have concerned themselves with the political conflicts of the Middle East. Look at the map below and answer the questions that follow.

1. Which country produces the most oil?
   _____
   _____

2. Which of the oil-producing nations produces the least oil?
   _____
   _____

3. Rank in order the remaining six countries shown on the map, placing the countries that produce the most oil at the top of the list.
   _____
   _____
   _____
   _____
   _____
   _____

4. Make a cartogram version of this map, using rectangles to show the shape and location of each country. The size of the countries should be based on the amount of oil they produce. Use Iraq, which produces about 100 million metric tons of oil per year, as your base. The sizes of the other countries should be related to the amount of oil they produce compared to Iraq. (You can look at page 671 of your textbook for an explanation of cartograms.)

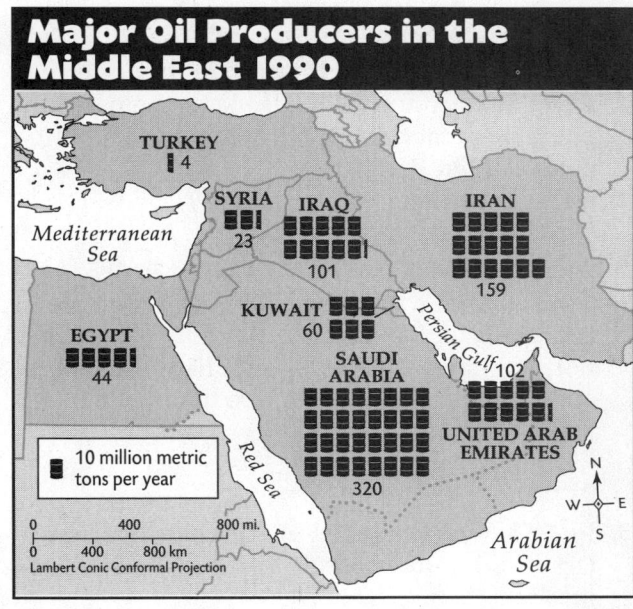

Major Oil Producers in the Middle East 1990

TURKEY 4
SYRIA 23
IRAQ 101
IRAN 159
EGYPT 44
KUWAIT 60
SAUDI ARABIA 320
UNITED ARAB EMIRATES 102

10 million metric tons per year

0   400   800 mi.
0   400   800 km
Lambert Conic Conformal Projection

Cartogram

World History   Mapping History Activities   35

Name _____ Date _____ Class _____

MAPPING HISTORY Activity 36

Travels of a Revolutionary

"The duty of every revolutionary is to make the revolution," declared the famous Latin American revolutionary leader Ernesto "Che" Guevara. His commitment to revolutionary struggle took him throughout Latin America. Using what you have learned about Latin America in this chapter, name each country described below. Then trace Guevara's travels through Latin America.

1. Guevara was born in Rosario, in the eastern part of this country. As a teenager, he participated in street fights against supporters of dictator Juan Perón.

   _____

2. To escape serving in Perón's army, in 1953 Guevara and a friend took a 3,000-mile train trip north to this country. This country, located north of Guevara's homeland, had just experienced a popular revolution to nationalize foreign-owned mines.

   _____

3. In 1953 he participated in this country's agrarian reform movement, led by leftist president Jacobo Arbenz Guzmán.

   _____

4. During the 1950s, Guevara joined a number of leftist movements throughout South America. He continued to travel northward through Peru, Ecuador, Panama, Costa Rica, and Guatemala. In 1955 Guevara met up with the exiled Fidel Castro, who was now living in this country. Years later in this same country, Native American peasants calling themselves Zapatistas would rebel against the government.

   _____

5. Guevara joined Castro and helped in the overthow of the dictator Fulgenico Batista of this country in 1959.

   _____

6. In 1966 Guevara returned to the country named after the liberator Simón Bolívar to set up guerrilla forces. He was killed there by government forces in 1967.

   _____

36   Mapping History Activities   World History

Name .... Date .... Class ....

MAPPING HISTORY Activity 37

The Commonwealth of Independent States

Demands for self-rule swept the Soviet republics in the relaxed atmosphere of glasnost. These demands resulted, ultimately, in independence in many places. The map below shows the Commonwealth of Independent States (CIS), a loose association of independent republics that in 1991 took the place of the Soviet Union. Look at the map and complete the activities that follow.

Russia and the Independent Republics

1. Why do you think that the Russian republic dominated the former Soviet Union?

   _____

   _____

2. Shortly after the formation of the CIS, ethnic and regional conflicts, suppressed under strict Communist rule, resurfaced in war between Armenia and Azerbaijan and in civil war in Georgia, Moldova, and Tajikstan. Devise a symbol to show the conflicts described and revise the map and map key.

3. What additional site of conflict in the CIS is not shown on the map? Which republic shown on the map is near it?

   _____

   _____

World History   Mapping History Activities   **37**

ANSWERS

Mapping History Activity 1, p. 1
1. Africa and the Middle East
2. From the Middle East, *Homo sapiens* migrated northeast through Asia, crossed a land bridge at the Bering Strait into North America, then moved southeast through Central America into South America.
3. *Accept all reasonable symbols. Students should position symbols in the areas indicated in the activity:* West Africa—watermelon, rice; Southeast Asia—bananas, cucumbers, yams; Europe—cattle, grapes; China—soybeans; Central Asia—camels; Central America—avocados, maize, tomatoes; North America—turkeys, sunflowers, beans.

Mapping History Activity 2, p. 2
1. Eridu
2. Ebla
3. Sumer
4. a.–d. *Students should correctly add the given cities according to the map scale.*
   e. Sumer

Mapping History Activity 3, p. 3
1. They were located on the Mediterranean coast.
2. Cyprus is northwest of Jerusalem.
3. Phoenicia
4. David's kingdom extended about 250 miles long, about 150 miles wide.
5. *Students should draw a route from the Red Sea north to Byblos. The straightest route is about 260 miles.*

Mapping History Activity 4, p. 4
1. approximately 300 miles
2. from Scylla and Charybdis to Calypso's island
3. *Lines and arrows should trace a path from Troy, to Lotus-Eaters, to Cyclops, to Laestrigonians, to Circe, to Entrance to Underworld, to Sirens, to Scylla and Charybdis, to Helios, to Calypso, to Phaeacians, to Ithaca.*
4. Calypso's Island to the land of the Phaeacians, approximately 1,350 miles

5. from the Sirens to Scylla and Charybdis

Mapping History Activity 5, p. 5
1. about 1,300 miles (2,091 km)
2. 3
3. Europe, Africa, and Asia

Students' keys will vary. Be sure that students make each pattern/color distinct enough so the generals' territories can easily be distinguished.
4. Seleucus
5. Antigonius

Mapping History Activity 6, p. 6
1. Huns
2. Visigoths, Huns, Vandals, and Ostrogoths
3. Visigoths and Vandals
4. Vandals
5. *Check to make sure that, for each modern city listed, students have added the following Roman names:* Eburacum (York), Londonium (London), Bonna (Bonn), Singidunum (Belgrade), Magontiacum (Frankfurt), Siccia (Vienna), Olisipo (Lisbon), Aquincum (Budapest).

Mapping History Activity 7, p. 7
1. Ghana, Mali, Songhai
2. Niger River
3. Cairo, Tripoli, Fez

Students' maps should show trade routes connecting Timbuktu with Taghaza and Niani. A third route should connect Taghaza with Fez; students could show an arrow indicating the arrival in Fez of goods from Europe. Another route should begin in Timbuktu and follow the Niger River south, then across to Kano, El Fasher, and the Nile, where it leads north to Cairo. Finally, a route should begin in the Middle East and follow the Mediterranean coast to Tripoli. A route from Timbuktu via Ghat should meet it there.

Mapping History Activity 8, p. 8
1. Rock Edicts found throughout India today would be good markers of the extent of the Mauryan Empire's power and influence.

2. Both empires contained major river systems; the Mauryan contained the Indus and the Ganges while the Gupta contained the Ganges only. Large river systems (or another accessible water source) are important because they provide transportation, food, and irrigation for crops, which help sustain the people.
3. The land between the Ganges and the Indus was probably not as fertile as the river valleys surrounding the rivers; otherwise the Aryans would have expanded directly southward as well as to the east and west.
4. *Students should draw three trade routes:* from India to Ceylon, through the Strait of Malacca, to Southeast Asia; from India across the Himalayas to Central Asia; from India through the Khyber Pass towards Arabia and Rome.

Mapping History Activity 9, p. 9
1. approximately 2,000 miles
2. The Gobi and the Himalayas prevented the expansion of the empire to the north and south.
3. *Students should include three arrows tracing Wudi's advancements:* northeast to North Korea, south to Southeast Asia, and northwest encircling the Tarim Basin. *Students should label the western end of the Great Wall "Jade City" and label the Tarim Basin to the west of "Jade City." The area controlled by the Hsiung-nu was north of the Silk Road near the Tarim Basin.*

Mapping History Activity 10, page 10
1. about 850 miles
2. Black Sea; Mediterranean Sea
3. *Arrows on map indicating the battle routes should point from Constantinople to Ad Decimum; from Ad Decimum to Sicily, Sardinia, and Corsica; from Sicily to Naples, Rome, and Ravenna; from Durres to Split; and from Cartagena into Spain.*

Mapping History Activity 11, page 11
1. approximately 200 miles
2. approximately 600 miles
3. west
4. southeast
5. *The path should begin at Madinah, go northwest to the Red Sea, then along the coast of Africa, into Spain and France, ending at Tours.*
6. approximately 3,750 miles

Mapping History Activity 12, p. 12
1. approximately 900 miles; approximately 1,000 miles
2. approximately 75 days
3. approximately 85 days
4. approximately 107 days (approximately 1,250 miles)
5. *Students' routes should extend from Rome through Paris to London; from Ireland through London to Paris to Spain; and from London through Germany to Scandinavia.*

Mapping History Activity 13, p. 13
1. large areas in the southwest and two small areas in the north
2. a large area in the north and west, a narrow strip through the center, and a large area in the southeast
3. Agincourt, Crécy, Orléans
4. *Reims should be marked just above the C in Champagne. Students' routes should connect Orléans, Reims, and Calais.*

Mapping History Activity 14, p. 14
1. *Students should correctly label the major Asian language families on the corresponding areas of their maps.*
2. Borobudur: Austronesian; Nara: Altaic
3. *Students should infer that the Austronesian language family spread throughout the area because people traveling from island to island in boats most likely spread similar languages among the inhabitants of each island.*
4. By converting to Islam, people in Indonesia and central Asia would have had to read or recite the Quran, written in Arabic. In this way, the vocabulary and grammatical structures of Arabic may have gradually entered the languages spoken in Indonesia and central Asia.

Mapping History Activity 15, p. 15
1. *Students should select three distinct colors to represent Spanish, English, and French holdings and add these to the map key.*
2. *Using colors that match their map key, students should indicate the following holdings:*
Spain: northern South America, Central America, Mexico, and entire coast of Florida
England: most of New England and Long Island, except for its westernmost tip, Eastern shore of Chesapeake Bay

World History   Mapping History Activities   **39**

France: St. Lawrence River, Nova Scotia, Prince Edward Island, eastern New Brunswick
3. Southwest, lower Eastern Woodlands
4. Eastern Woodlands
5. Subarctic, Eastern Woodlands

Mapping History Activity 16, p. 16
1. 75 percent Catholic; 25 percent Protestant
2. circled in blue: Wittenberg, Worms, Zurich, Geneva, Münster; circled in red: Rome, Trent
3. *Answers will vary. Students may conclude that the Protestant Reformation was more successful in spreading Protestantism in urban areas, while the Catholic Reformation was more successful in rural areas. Remind students that geographical boundaries may have been at least partly responsible for either reformation's success.*

Mapping History Activity 17, p. 17
1. to Chaco Canyon
2. Zape to Rio Grande Pueblos
3. *Students' drawings should clearly distinguish the routes of the Cholula from that of the Teotihuacán and Tula. Lines should appear from Cholula to: the X on the west coast, the Y on the east coast, Casas Grandes to "Hohokam," and Casas Grandes to "Hopi."*

Mapping History Activity 18, p. 18
1. Europeans might use the inability of the Qing government to stop the Taiping unrest promptly as an excuse to intervene with military forces in order to protect their own people. The Qing, they might argue, were unable to protect their own people from violence, so how could they protect European foreigners?
2. about 570 miles from Nanking to southern border of Taiping-dominated territory
3. Hung may have gotten his Christian training from European missionaries located in one of the Canton ports in southern China.
4. *Students should shade the area along the coast from Canton north to Shanghai.*

Mapping History Activity 19, p. 19
1. The Hapsburgs owned significant lands throughout Europe, including valuable harbors in the Netherlands, Spain, and Italy.
2. *Answers will vary. Possible response:* Yes, since doing so made it very difficult for Philip II to supervise his far-flung holdings, especially the Netherlands, Milan, and Sardinia.
3. *Answers will vary. Possible response:* A central location such as the border of the Holy Roman Empire in France might have been better because it would have provided better access to all of the empire's holdings.
4. *Possible response:* France, because Philip II could have moved on three fronts: north from Spain, south from the Netherlands, and west from central Europe
5. *Students should draw the borders of present-day France, Spain, Belgium, Germany, the Netherlands, the Czech Republic, Switzerland, etc., using the Reference Atlas. Students should realize that Spain, Portugal, and France are essentially the same configuration. The Netherlands are now smaller. Italy is larger. Belgium, the Czech Republic, Austria, Hungary, Slovenia, Croatia, Slovakia, and Germany have since been created.*

Mapping History Activity 20, p. 20
1. *Answers may include:* Germany, Bosnia-Herzegovina, Albania, Slovenia, Italy, Czech Republic, Slovakia, Austria, Hungary, Croatia, Belgium, Luxembourg. *Students may point out that the boundaries of many nations that existed in the Age of Enlightenment have changed.*
2. *Answers may include:* Paris, London, Rome, Madrid, and Amsterdam.
3. *Students should mark and label Kraków, Rome, London, Paris, and England.*

Mapping History Activity 21, p. 21
1. *One dotted line should begin at the St. Lawrence River, go to Lake Ontario and across to Oswego, then to the Mohawk River. The other dotted line should begin at New York City and go north along the Hudson River. The solid line should begin at Montreal, go to the Hudson River, then south along the river.*
2. 200 miles (322 kilometers)
3. 75 miles (121 kilometers)
4. *Students should identify Howe's route as the easiest because it involved sailing upriver and marching through a river valley.*

Mapping History Activity 22, p. 22
1. a. 1812
   b. France, the Netherlands, the Italian states, Poland
   c. Spain, Norway, Denmark, the Austrian Empire

40 Mapping History Activities   World History

2. Great Britain, Portugal, Sweden, the Ottoman Empire, Russia, Sardinia, Sicily
3. a. *Map symbols should be appropriate, placed in the map key, and labeled.*
   b. *Students should mark battles at the following points on the map:* Marengo—approx. 1/2 inch NW of Rome; Trafalgar—just off Cape Trafalgar; Austerlitz—approx. 7/16 inch SW of Warsaw; Auerstedt—just SW of Leipzig; Jena—just SE of Auerstedt; Friedland—extreme northern Poland, approx. 3/16 inch from Baltic Sea; Peninsular War—Spain; Wagram—just N of Vienna; Aspern—just NE of Vienna; Borodino—about 3/16 inch W of Moscow; Lützen—about 3/16 inch W of Leipzig; Leipzig—at Leipzig; Ligny—about 3/16 inch SE of Waterloo; Waterloo—at Waterloo
   c. *Answers will vary but should be supported with explanations. Students who agree will likely refer to the number of battles and their locations at many places in Europe. Students who disagree may point out that most places in Europe were not battle sites.*

Mapping History Activity 23, p. 23

1. Exeter, Bath, Norwich, Leeds, and Manchester
2. around Newcastle in northeast England and in the area from Leeds to just south of Sheffield
3. a canal
4. the Humber River
5. *Routes will vary, but should minimize overland distance and utilize canals and rivers between Bath and London and Birmingham and London.*

Mapping History Activity 24, p. 24

1. The Galápagos Islands are a little over 500 miles (805 kilometers) from the mainland.
2. *Students should show a course following the description given in the exercise.*

Mapping History Activity 25, p. 25

1. 1800–1810, 1841–1850
2. 1821–1830, 1831–1840
3. Lands the United States acquired after 1860 were not entirely within the mainland of the United States.
4. Both maps show the United States expansion of territory during the 1800s. The map on page 664 of the textbook indicates how the territory was acquired. *Students' maps should emphasize the order in which territory was acquired, combining acquisitions by decade. For instance, this second map shows more clearly the fact that Florida was acquired in stages over two decades.*

Mapping History Activity 26, p. 26

1. Austria, Tyrol, near Bohemia
2. Prague
3. *Students' symbols will vary. Industrial symbols should appear in Bohemia and Moravia; agricultural symbols should appear in Hungary.*

Mapping History 27, p. 27

1. the north and the west
2. coal, gold, diamonds, copper, uranium
3. *Answers will vary but may be similar to the following:*
   1: Great Britain. Although Britain did not have as much territory as France, the southern and western colonies were rich in natural resources.
   2: France. Covering the most landmass, France had strong holdings of natural gas and petroleum but lacked some precious materials and minerals.
   3: Germany. Even though Germany did not have extensive holdings in Africa, its territory in southern Africa was very rich in most resources except natural gas and petroleum.
   4: Portugal. With the exception of some petroleum and diamonds, the landholdings of Portugal did not yield many natural resources.

Mapping History Activity 28, p. 28

1. Romania, Serbia, Montenegro, Albania, Greece
2. because Gallipoli lay at a strategic point—at an opening of a seaway leading directly to Constantinople, the capital of the Ottoman Empire
3. They could then join their territory and move to assert control over the entire Balkan Peninsula.
4. a. *Arrows should point to Serbia from Sofia and Belgrade.*
   b. *Students should shade Austria-Hungary.*
   c. *Arrows should point to Budapest and Constantinople from Greece.*

Mapping History Activity 29, p. 29
Students' keys and arrows should be appropriately color-coded.
1. *One arrow should point from Greece to Turkey, and another arrow should point from Turkey to Greece.*
2. *Arrows should point from Romania to Turkey, from Bulgaria to Turkey, and from Yugoslavia to Turkey.*
3. *Arrows should point from northern Poland to Germany, from southern Poland to Germany, from Czechoslovakia to Germany, and from northeast France to Germany.*
4. *Arrows should point from Germany to Belgium, to the Netherlands, to France, to Switzerland, and across the Atlantic.*
5. *Arrows should point to Hungary from Romania, from northern Yugoslavia, and from eastern Czechoslovakia.*

Mapping History Activity 30, p. 30
Students will not be able to show the exact route from the description provided, but they should indicate the general direction (west, then north, then northeast) of the march and the area covered.
1. mostly mountainous
2. approximately 900 miles (1,450 kilometers)
3. The army was fighting as it retreated, and these changes in direction could have been caused by battles.

Mapping History Activity 31, p. 31
1. In 1942, Spain, Portugal, Switzerland, and Sweden were all neutral.
2. the Soviet Union
3. *Arrows should point from New York to locations in Europe, from Virginia to India, from Seattle to Aleutian Islands, from San Francisco to several locations in the Pacific, and from Los Angeles to India.*

Mapping History Activity 32, p. 32
1. *Answers will vary. Possible answer:* Finland and Austria bordered Warsaw Pact members and thus probably believed that their security lay in remaining neutral.
2. *Students should use a colored pencil and draw the Iron Curtain from the Baltic Sea along the eastern border of the Federal Republic of Germany, Austria, and Italy to the Adriatic Sea, indicating its color on the map key.*

Mapping History 33, p. 33
Answers will vary but should be similar to the following:
1. There is a narrow band of crops that are produced in the north, but most of the crop production occurs in central to southeast China.
2. Cattle and domesticated animals are most likely raised in the "grazing lands" that are located across the northern and western portions of China.
3. A map that labels specific products is more precise than a map which shades agricultural regions. It also gives readers the opportunity to make more specific inferences about other aspects of life in the area shown. For example, by considering the crops that are grown in a particular region, one can infer details about the region's climate, its elevation, and the lives of its inhabitants.

Mapping History Activity 34, p. 34
1. The densest vegetation is found in the rainforest regions along the west coast of Africa and the east coast of Madagascar. The least vegetation is found in the desert areas, roughly the wide band that runs through north-central Africa and widens as it moves east.
2. It appears that the savanna covers the most territory, while the temperate grassland covers the least.
3. *Answers will vary. Possible answer:* It is likely that the small northern and southern band of Mediterranean-type vegetation would yield the highest return of crops, as Mediterranean regions have particularly rich soil and abundant crops.
4. *Students will mark areas near the Nile River, Lake Victoria, Mediterranean coastline, coastline from Senegal to Nigeria, eastern coastline of South Africa.*
5. Most areas of dense population are in Mediterranean vegetation zones. An exception to this pattern is in northeastern Africa in a desert region, along the Nile River. This indicates that populations develop near areas with good vegetation and water supplies. Some areas may have a high population density due to employment opportunities. For example, cities offer many jobs in manufacturing and service industries.
6. *Answers will vary. Possible answer:* Access to land, natural resources, employment

opportunities, and family relationships may all influence where a person lives.

Mapping History Activity 35, p. 35
1. Saudi Arabia
2. Turkey
3. Iran, United Arab Emirates, Iraq, Kuwait, Egypt, Syria
4. *Cartograms should show Saudi Arabia as the biggest country and Turkey as the smallest country. Kuwait should be about three-fifths the size of Iraq, Egypt should be just under one-half, Syria should be just under one-quarter, and Turkey should be about one-twentieth the size of Iraq. The United Arab Emirates should be about the same size, but its shape will be different. Iran should be about one and one-half times the size of Iraq, and Saudi Arabia should be about three and one-fifth times the size of Iraq. To summarize, the following countries should be smaller than they appear on the base map: Turkey, Syria, Egypt, Iran, United Arab Emirates. Kuwait should appear larger. Iraq and Saudi Arabia will stay the same size they are shown on the base map. The shapes of all the countries will change to create a cartogram.*

Mapping History Activity 36, p. 36
1. Argentina
2. Bolivia
3. Guatemala
4. Mexico
5. Cuba
6. Bolivia

Students should trace Guevara's route through Latin America as described in the activity.

Mapping History Activity 37, p. 37
1. *Answers will vary. Possible answer:* Russia dominated the Soviet Union because, as the largest republic, it probably had the most people and the most national resources.
2. *Students should devise a symbol to show, on the map and in the map key, the conflicts described. For example, the symbol could be a weapon placed on the border of warring republics and within republics where civil wars occurred, or students could cover war areas with a pattern such as wavy lines or dots.*
3. Chechnya is not shown. It is near the border between Russia and Georgia.

ACKNOWLEDGMENTS

Maps
Cartographic Services provided by Ortelius Design, and
Joe LeMonnier